MARRIAGE MOATS

MARRIAGE MOATS

Published and printed in the United States of America by
Fountain Publishing, P.O. Box 80011, Rochester, Michigan 48308

Cover photo by Chara Odhner

Book design by Karin Alfelt Childs
Set in Palatino
ISBN 10: 1936665085
ISBN 13: 978-1-936665-08-2

Marriage Moats

101 Thoughts to Inspire and Protect Your Marriage

LORI S. ODHNER

 FOUNTAIN PUBLISHING®

Dedication:
I offer my humble and copious thanks to my husband John for his continual support for writing these stories. His willingness to let our life spill into the pages, in the hope that they might be stepping stones for others, makes me love him all the more.

Contents

Welcome

Welcome to Marriage Moats!

My son Benjamin has autism. His latest recurring question is about moats. He asks "What is a moat?" eager to hear again what he already knows.

"A moat is water that surrounds a castle and keeps it safe from enemies."

He smiles, and asks what enemies are.

"They are people who want to hurt you."

He wanders off into a memory about moats in movies he has seen, and laughs about bad guys who fell into them.

People sometimes say that a person's home is his or her castle. Marriage can be a castle, but that does not mean it is never under attack.

I am intrigued by the idea of a moat, as a deterrent for flame flinging masked marauders.

This book is called *Marriage Moats*, because it offers a modest obstacle to those influences that undermine marriage. It will provide a puddle of protection in the form of a quote, or anecdote. You can choose to read a story that may surround your mental fortress with a waterway that keeps you safer. Water is like truth, in that it keeps you clean and quenched, and paired with a boat, gets you to places you would be hard pressed to find otherwise. Truth can transport you to resorts as well, places of refuge, and beauty.

Marriage Moats is one wet barrier you can create to stave off the armies of negativity and apathy that incessantly bash on your door.

You may even find it funny to watch the critical thoughts splashing and thrashing, unable to reach you, while you watch from a turret in the clouds.

Lori Odhner

The Moats

In Love

Dear Lord,

Can I capture this feeling and hold on to it always?? I am in love!! The explosion of joy, and silliness is popping out of me. The birds are singing and so am I.

Can I take a picture of this feeling and bring it out on days when my heart has forgotten, as a promise that those feelings will return? When they feel like they are gone, are they really gone, or just tucked away like sweaters in summer?

Buttons

Why do we want that row of tiny buttons on the back of a wedding dress? Zippers would be faster, or velcro for that matter. Buttons take time to sew on, to fasten, to undo. Yet for many people, a wedding is not about hurrying.

There is time that goes into the dating process, into the decision to marry. There are some traditions that are purposely slow. The way the wedding party saunters up the aisle may embody lovely attributes...elegance, unity, family. But haste is not one of them. Except for the overeager ring bearer who forgets all instructions and bolts, the journey is a mindful stroll.

Perhaps the pace is an effort to take in all the faces and feelings of the ten score cousins and coworkers, roommates and grandmothers who have donned their best earrings and made travel plans months in advance to be here, now with this couple. Each person feels the connecting heartstrings of heredity, history, and high school that gives him or her the right to attend this celebration. Everyone wants to be close enough to smell the roses, to hear their vows, to taste the frosting.

There is, miraculously, enough joy to go around. No matter how many relatives crowd into the pews, the bride's splendor is not diminished by more misty eyes. The organ and strings are no less resonant for being shared by four hundred ears. There is no visible drain on the couple's ability to smile at each well wisher during the reception.

What began as a crescendoing climax, a gift to and also from the hundreds of people who are present, sometimes tragically ends in solitude.

When couples struggle, they hide.

The agony lies in the fact that all those people who came with sparkly gifts and spilling hearts did not disappear. They still care.

Imagine if instead of a series of strained phone calls and letters from attorneys, the course of action for a stumbling marriage harnessed the collective power of that wedding years past. Imagine if you sent out invitations to an identical guest list, to climb on planes and into cars to come and offer support. This time, instead of being the iridescent center of the festivities, the couple could slump in as an empty cup, needing to be filled. People could compose messages, read aloud for all to hear. Memories, photographs and stories would nourish the hurting husband and wife. Like in the movie "It's a Wonderful Life" each loving person could express what this marriage means to them before it dies, what would have been lost if it had never been.

I wish that there were hundreds of tiny buttons, fastening us into this covenant. I wish that the exit was slower. Marriages can split apart as fast as a zipper, demanding children to velcro back and forth between parents.

If we could let those people near enough to see the tears, hear the pain, taste the failure, the buttons just might stay closed.

Fire Spinning

This is my husband. Isn't he brave?

He has leashed the power of fire and is spinning it in rapid circles around his highly combustible body. If a horde of masked bandits were pilfering in the neighborhood about now, I bet they would resist the urge to pick his pockets. It would not be worth the danger to cross those flames. They would look for a less protected victim.

John does a stellar job of keeping our marriage safe too. He shuns adultery.

For years I had no clue why he even bothered. He had me, his adoring wife, so why did he need to worry about being attracted to other women? It is not that I imagined myself to be dazzlingly beautiful, it is just that I thought his decision had been made, signed and sealed and the temptation was over.

I was wrong.

Twenty years of oblique conversations finally got through to me. Staying faithful is work. Of course it might not be such intense work, if women dressed differently, or the standards of behavior in movies had not eroded to the point where PG now means Pretty Graphic.

Marriages are highly combustible, and we have all been witness to the pain of watching them go up in flames.

It is labor he does alone. Standing strong inside a ring of fire, protected by prayer and the determination to keep the relationship bandits at bay, John has kept our marriage whole. I do not know how to do the fire spinning for him. But I can say thank you.

He is my hero.

Carrots

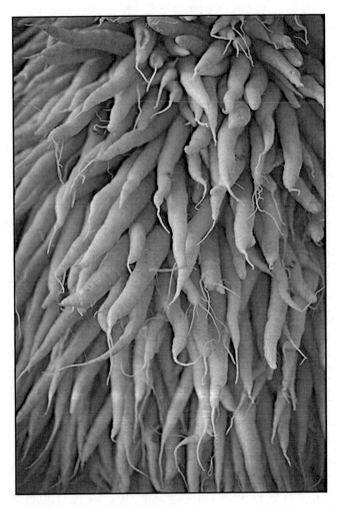

Carrots are a humble food.

They make a good show above ground, with lacy greens like a fountain springing from brown earth. But the part that feeds you is hidden away from marauding rabbits and misguided lawn mowers.

Embryonic carrots start at the surface and go deep, deeper. Orange appears like magic from a seed that had no more pigment than dryer lint, and is scarcely the size of a cookie crumb.

You rarely see commercials for carrots, though they are as

deserving of recognition as the latest spill proof yogurt snack. They are versatile, showing up in organic salads, daal, stir fries, thick soups, juice, juliennes and cream cheese frosted cake.

I like that there are usually carrots in our vegetable crisper. They do not have the snazzy packaging of a resealable zip lock bag, and there is probably even some residual dirt, waiting to be scrubbed.

But they are crunchy, and sweet, and do good things for my body if I let them. Eating them gives me keener eyesight, higher B-carotene levels, and antioxidants. Even kids who wish I would bring them salt and vinegar potato chips while they play on the floor accept the offering of carrot sticks, and when I come back the bowl is empty.

Marriage is nourishing too, when your soul feels hungry for the companionship of someone who has come to stay. Dating and a string of relationships can be an energy drain... questions and indecision that show up too frequently when all you want is to know.

Falling in love was fun, I will admit, and as pretty as the carrot tops flirting in the breeze. But what keeps me alive, today, next year, is the part you cannot see. It is the taproot that reaches for the core, finding minerals where my eyes cannot even go and bringing them back to me as lunch.

God hides good things in secret places, and my marriage seems to attract them. We work together to carry sleepy children in from the car after a long trip home from the shore, and have a conversation about our floundering son. We practice listening, when it is neither easy nor convenient to do so. Our vision gets keener, our compassion levels climb, and we are better able to ward off relational disease. These are like vitamins, hidden in the soil of life, that add vitality to a spiritual body that would atrophy on a diet of deliciously deceptive self indulgence.

We are courted by the media with a far different message, one that props narcissism as irresistibly as it does freeze pops, neither of which are even close to being food.

So bring on the carrots. I have some cream cheese and nuts. Today, I want to make cake.

Wishing

What do you wish for? Do you even believe in wishing?

I pray with my twins each night. Praying is a cousin of wishing. Wishes are letters sent with no address, just lots of pretty stamps. Prayers are precisely addressed to God.

Something tender happens when I pray with my girls. They listen. There is no editing on their part, but sometimes they cannot keep their questions quiet, and they ask.

"Why are you sorry about what you said to your sister?"

"What happened to Martha that you are praying for her?"

"I didn't know your back hurts, Mama. I am so sorry."

Sometimes they add their prayers to my stamp too, regardless of whether they know who Ethan and Jessica are.

My girls pray for their marriages every night. They have kept it up for three years. They each ask to be a good wife, and they pray for their husbands to be good fathers.

Praying with someone you love makes you vulnerable. Even though my daughters have a perfect history of not judging me, I still falter as I admit my wrongs aloud. Their eyes are closed, but their hearts are open. It is a miracle every time.

The 12 step program suggests that admitting our faults to another human being is part of the road to spiritual well being. Walking it with someone who cares for you brightens the path with candlelight.

Really?

What kind of optimist plants a seed the size of a baby's toe and actually believes it will grow into a giant sunflower? Just because the package says so? I notice that no one is willing to stick his neck out and sign the instructions, so that you could come asking for a refund if it is a dud.

Yet apparently people keep buying them and poking them into the dirt with lofty hopes of golden petals playing ring around the rosy with a chocolate center.

I am dubious. I mean, I could rip it out of the ground, dissect it, even peer at it through a microscope and not see a hint of yellow. As for size, who swallows the idea of a one inch pair of leaves barely big enough to cast a shadow defying gravity and the conservation of mass to multiply in height by a factor of 143?

Ok, ok, I will give it some time. Three or four hours. Maybe a whole day. But if I do not see results by tomorrow, Friday at the latest, I am outta here.

Actually, the seedling is doing a stellar job. In the world of vegetation, speed is not the only consideration. Color, resilience, texture and fragrance score points too. Porous ground, enough water and warmth help a lot. I once speed read a scientific study whose premise was that yelling makes plants more susceptible to failure.

What kind of Pollyanna believes that a seedling relationship will grow into a beautiful flowering one? Just because God says it can?

Couples keep showing up to get married, even though, if you take them apart, you cannot find the qualities that the package advertises: wisdom, compatibility, mutual desire to do each other every good.

Do I really believe that this friendship, now measured in a fistful of months, will grow into a relationship that fills half a century? Can something no bigger than a promise expand to include children and grandchildren playing ring around the rosy, homes mortgaged and lived in, problems weathered together, parents buried, tears spilled and felt? A colorful life includes a palette of mournful gray, joyful lemon yellow, reflective sage green, and passionate scarlet.

And come to think of it, I think yelling makes us more susceptible to failure too.

What kind of Pollyanna believes that a seedling relationship will grow into a beautiful flowering one? Just because God says it can?

Me.

Colly

I still love my colander, the one I got as a shower gift in 1980. I confess I cannot remember who gave it to me, but I would wager that the giver has forgotten too. I do remember the light banter as my cousin Chara wrote down each gift in her expressive and curly cursive, so I could write proper thank yous, and the question about its correct spelling.

Colly has traveled with me to five homes in four states and three time zones. If she could talk, she would tell you about the frequency of spaghetti being served, and the sensation of steaming pasta and cool water colliding in her bowled embrace. She would perhaps comment on the color change when our diet shifted from whole wheat to corn noodles, and finally settled on brown rice. Colly might feel honored to have overheard the hundreds of blessings offered over her humble fare.

Some things slip through our remembrance.... as well they should. Keeping score of who got up with the baby, or who took out the garbage robs us of the food that really nourishes us. What is left behind are the hearty memories of shared meals and playful conversations. The annoyances that are rinsed away leave us cleaner, cooler.

Drop in sometime on a Thursday. We will probably be just starting to spill the sauce and shake the Parmesan. Come early enough to hold hands for the blessing. It is always a good idea to give a proper thank you.

Sleep My Love

Everyone sleeps.

If someone is not sleeping, they make noises about it to anyone who will listen, because in the absence of complete rest, we crumble.

There is something tender about sharing this vulnerable time with your spouse. Your guard is down, you disengage with your surroundings, your heart rate slips into an easy rhythm. The blood supply to your muscles increases, and your body has a chance to heal.

When my children worry about a small cut, I reassure them that God fixes hurts when our eyes are closed, to keep His work a secret.

Marriages sleep too. They sway between fierce and frantic activity that jumbles and bumbles through our extended days, and slumping into bed for those truncated nights.

But God is efficient with the scant hours in which we submit to His safekeeping. Some marriages simply heal.

I have read studies that track unhappy marriages over time. In a surprising number of them, five years after reporting that they are dissatisfied with their relationship, husbands and wives respond differently. They tell the researchers that they are now content. This is not always a result of counseling or drastic changes. Sometimes couples just grow.

I know I did. I used to complain about things that seemed unconscionable to me a few years into the game. Once I ranted to a friend that John had clipped all the oleander bushes and left the trimmings where they lay. Didn't she think that was terrible? She paused.

"Well at our house I do the trimming and the picking up," was all she said. Unfinished gardening fell off my list of unforgivable sins.

At another turning point I was rock certain that John's tendency to not hand in receipts meant that he does not love me. I built a frenetic case of righteousness in my mind. Then I let it go for awhile. I slept on it for a year or so. Now I am calmer about it. I try to rescue the receipts from his email and pockets and submit them. He has not really changed. I have.

Sometimes we need to close our eyes and let God do the healing.

Just a Juice Box

Why is it so easy to be content when you are two years old? It is not as if there is no material for concern. Who knows if this little guy's daddy will lose his job next week, or his mother may fall carrying laundry and break both legs. It happens. Then there are global problems. Foreclosure is rampant, his generation will be crushed by the national debt, and if he had any ambitions of being a shrimp fisherman in the Gulf, well forget it.

But he looks pretty satisfied with just a juice box.

Now it is not as if I am from some other planet and have missed the notorious behavior of thwarted preschoolers. I have escaped from my share of grocery stores with a flailing child in my arms. I got a black eye when my second son threw a book at me.

But there is another side of small people that is so subtle it can go unnoticed. They can be happy with what is.

I had a little girl who carried on a conversation with her shoelaces in the car on a long trip. I took a little boy to the thrift store and he was positively joyful to find a key chain shaped like a pickle.

There is a quality about young children that leaves me speechless. They choose the parents they have. If I were in a line up of fifty women that included heiresses, rock stars, Fortune 500 entrepreneurs and Minnie Mouse, my baby would pick me every time. Even if I had recently declared a ban on sweetened cereal. Kids are on occasion incensed by the lunch menu or the absence of popsicles, but ask for a Mommy upgrade? Never.

God gave him this mother and father, and he is not trading.

Wives and husbands are not always like this.

I like hanging with small folk. They are good role models.

The Tail

I do not understand physics enough to know why planes need tails. I have heard that aircraft fly better with them attached, as do kites and helicopters, and even birds. I like that they still work in cloudy weather and at night.

Maybe it has to do with holding the airplane on course. Wings are handy for keeping you aloft, although I don't exactly comprehend that either. John and I went to a science museum with our kids and played with mega fans and plastic arm wings. I felt the invisible force that lifted me, and learned that it is true in a way I had only borrowed belief for before, though I still am a long way from understanding.

Perhaps Orville and Wilbur suffered a few crashes before they added tails to their design. I wonder if they ever tried to tape one on mid flight, when things were getting wobbly. After that they would have known that it is best to weld it on tightly before you start the engine.

The nose of the plane has every intention of going forward, but sans tail it can start to yaw and pitch. I find it intriguing that a limb perched in the rear of the plane can influence the front.

I have been told that planes fly fast, though the paradox is that while I am standing in the cabin of a 747 I can easily be persuaded that we are stationary. I glance out the window for a reference point, to prove to myself that we are indeed moving, but the fields and buildings seem impossibly far away.

My marriage sometimes feels like a plane 30,000 feet up. We are careening through space at a breakneck speed, carrying our children, our dreams and some baggage. There are ideas that I fastened to my relation-ship before I took off.

"True marriage love is the most excellent of all uses, for from it is the procreation of the human race and from the human race, the angelic heaven."
Emanuel Swedenborg, *Marriage Love* 183

Those twenty eight words have influenced my direction and increased my elevation. They echo in my brain when I cannot find the way through the clouds that obscure my vision. I say them to myself when everything is pitch black, to steady my relationships from yawing and pitching off course. The quote was part of my take off, and when I feel unsure of where I am headed I look over my shoulder to see if it is still there. It always is. I don't fancy trying to attach it mid flight.

The thought, riveted to my being, calibrates our destination and the reason for getting there. Sometimes I try to find visible proof that I am indeed headed in the direction of raising angels, but the celestial landscape feels distant. I am easily duped that we are standing still.

I don't understand how wings and tails work. But I do know that I need them.

Something Good

It takes a trained eye to spy something good.

A sloppy gaze can easily find the broken, annoying, worn out things. Noticing the ache in your shoulders comes easily. Awareness of your pain free joints does not. Who starts a conversation with what is working well?

"Hey, my car started this morning!"

"Our teenage son was friendly at dinner."

"My husband came home last night after work!"

Yet those circumstances are part of our experience too. It takes effort to see them, to acknowledge them and to be grateful for them.

One of the regular parts of the marriage group we lead is called "Brag Time." In it, we invite people to tell the gang something they love about their spouse. It is fun. I have noticed that some couples cannot muster the words to appreciate this person beside them. I can almost see their gratitude door rusted shut. They listen for the first few weeks, as others tell stories about how their partner let them sleep in, or built a new fence, or took the cranky kids to the park.

Then, like the Tin Man, the oil of love and a little motion creaks it open, and they too have a new heart.

Sometimes people arrive at marriage group in a fractious condition. They have spent the better part of the day chasing toddlers, or placating customers. But here they are now in a comfortable chair, with the person they eagerly chose to spend the rest of their life with. Then after a few minutes of listening to the everyday kindnesses of other ordinary marriages, they smile. The stress of the commute loses its grip. There is room for contentment, even more when you push aside the cobwebby complaints.

What person starts a conversation with what is working well? A trained one.

Cable Knits

Where are your sweaters? You probably know. Some people store them in the attic, or in plastic bags in the basement. Others hide them in cedar chests or in boxes under the bed with the dust bunnies.

I have never noticed anyone who, in a flurry of spring cleaning, chucks all the winter garb. Experience tells us that no matter how sweltering August may feel, frosty mornings are in our not too distant future.

So we take the challenge head on and buy sweaters... maybe

even a handmade Irish cable knit, or an apricot cashmere for special occasions. We need to have a strategy for retaining body heat in January so we may as well make it pretty.

Marital heat has a way of escaping too, when the wintry blasts scour through the rafters. I have neighbors that know how to get ready. On the anniversary of the death of their daughter they prepare a special day.... canoeing in a river, volunteering at Ronald McDonald house, building a play structure for their grandchildren. Instead of letting the painful memories chill them to the bone, they bundle up, plan ahead and fill the emptiness with good things.

My family of origin had a secret weapon too. One of the struggles we trudged through was an income that hovered a little above the poverty line. I have almost no memories of buying new clothes, and certainly none of vacations involving anything more expensive than gas to Aunt Muriel's house in Maine, but whenever he could find a candle to light and a dessert to serve, my father would say, "We're havin' a party!"

It worked, by the way. When he said those four words, with a smile I can still render up, I was suddenly transported to a celebration in our own dimmed livingroom with nothing more than people and Boston cream pie.

John has his own version of the warmies. When we are doing something that we actually agreed we enjoy doing, but I am too caught up to notice, he says, "Does this count?" It can be as ordinary as chopping vegetables together, or singing in the evening by the piano. It may be as spare as looking up at the clouds on a brisk fall afternoon, or the sweetness of two girls curled up reading on the couch.

It may not be angora, but it keeps us warm.

Meet Me at the Cafe

When was the last time you met your spouse for coffee? I know, I know, there is coffee at home. And there is the babysitting issue, and money is tight. But all that aside, when was the last time?

A few weeks ago John and I actually planned to go out together. This is not normal behavior for us, but we did it anyway. I arranged for childcare and even had a place in mind. Then we got in a tiff. I did not really want to go out with him anymore. Why spend good money to argue when we could do it for free at home?

But something I cannot quite put my finger on pushed me to get in the car, not talking much, and drive to the cafe. We stood in line and ordered, and sat down at one of those little tables where neither of you can actually hide. It was almost as stilted as a date back in high school, only clammier.

Then the food came, and we paid attention to our entrees. I bumped a glass and he caught it before it fell. We held hands for the blessing, because tiff or no tiff that is what we do.

Forgetting that I was supposed to be aloof, I started to tell him about my day. He listened, in a way that he has developed over the years and could not help but resurface even in the current emotional weather.

He smiled. I softened. The Issue started to lose its grip as a headline, and we were bantering about something much more interesting.

I lost myself in the moment, in the time together, in the familiarity of being with someone who has seen me chew with my mouth open. He has watched me misbehave and not bailed. How can that not be precious? How can I treat him more carelessly than someone else's dishware?

It was an ordinary lunch date. But then again, not so much.

Training Wheels

Ours is a culture that buys the idea of offering support....
training wheels, internships, graduate advisers, computer manu-
als, cookbooks. There is a belief that if you help someone get started, they will write better dissertations and make lighter souffles.
So where does the support show up in marriage? Who is model-
ing good communication skills and verbal appreciations?

Once, just because I was curious, I counted how many air
breathing couples I witnessed interacting with each other in a
positive way for a week. The conversation had to be longer than

two sentences, to register on my low budget research project. I was shocked, but then again I wasn't. The total number of marital exchanges was... zero.

Now granted I do not still live with my parents, who managed plenty of friendly interactions in between the bi polar driven ones. For many people childhood is the only place they ever had a front row seat on couple dynamics. If, by chance, their parent's marriage ranked in the top 20%, great. One role model is better than none. But if that marriage was rocky or dismantled, it leaves a gaping hole where memories of conflict resolution, affection and cooperation are supposed to take up residence.

But there are good marriages out there. They do not manage to get as much media attention as the Hollywood wife of the month club does. You have to look for them. I have found them on quiet walks in the cool of the evening, or touching heads in church. I have heard their laughter at wedding receptions, and seen their misty glances at graduations. Ironically, many of them do not really think of themselves as noteworthy. Their marriage is something that has grown up around them, carrying them above their own needs and failings. They do not think of themselves as front page news any more than a person with a flabby but functioning body expects to be on the cover of Fitness magazine.

I invite you, if you have a marriage that keeps you smiling at least on an intermittent basis, to go ahead and have a conversation in front of innocent bystanders. Talk about why you fell in love, or how you resolve taking turns with the garbage, or something sweet your husband did for you. It may feel brazen. But then again you may have just helped a young bride, or future bridegroom learn how to balance without training wheels.

Back From the Office

I am grateful that my husband goes to work every day. We did not really pin that detail down when we were dating.

"You will consistently earn an income for the next forty years or so." But it has come in rather handy for covering routine expenses.

Sometimes I think the sheer longevity of that expectation has taken a toll on him. There were times in his career when walking through the door at work took grit. He has had his share of criticism, and sometimes the job requirements were not based in reality.

It is not that I was exactly goofing off either. I was after all answering endless questions involving "Why?" and making macaroni for nine children. We even homeschooled for a decade. But being the basically ego centric person that I have been, I was more acutely aware of my Herculean efforts than I was of his.

Looking back, I am trying to proffer thanks retroactively.

"John, I appreciate your continual efforts to provide for our family. Your commitment to give us a home, safety, food and clothing is a gift to all of us. I respect you, and I love you."

"You are going to work tomorrow too, right?"

Call Me

More.

The little boy in this photograph is using sign language to tell the ocean that he wants more waves. I am not sure if the seas are multilingual. Considering the fact that they lap on international shores, it would be good if they were.

Husbands can sometimes be in the background of a marriage duo. They may not be the one who does the inviting, or remembers birthdays. They may talk less at a dinner party, or prefer to stay at home. My own hubby can be pretty chatty if the topic involves Macs or lasers. But when the conversation rolls around to feelings, he gets quieter.

He has explained to me that men's brains have more gray matter, and women's brains more white. It has to do with men having a harder time getting the words and emotions in sync. Men certainly have feelings. But corralling them into syllables is trickier than keeping a wave on the shore.

It is a little like the difference between how my adult children use the phone and how I did back in high school. I lived in a dormitory with fifty other girls and to make a call you had to find loose change on your dresser, go down two flights of stairs to the lobby, wait for a turn, insert a dime and hope your mom would accept the charges, dial the eleven rotating digits, pray that the line was not busy and then if she answered.... talk. When any of my six oldest children want to speak to me they scoop the phone out of their pocket and lightly touch speed dial. If that is too much effort they can just say "Call Mom."

I had plenty to say when I was sixteen, but the path to being able to express it when I was a hundred miles from home was tedious. My husband, too has things to say, but it takes work.

It is easy to notice the little girl jumping waves. She would be quick to tell you how much fun she is having. The little boy has his own experience of the ocean. But to find out about it you may need to be willing to silence your own reaction and learn sign language.

Slipping Away

Oh Lord,

The light is slipping away. It was bright a few hours or years ago, so lavishly the intensity rendered me squinting. I could see nothing but promise as the heat of the noontime sun baked against my browning skin.

But now the sun is leaving me behind, and takes my clarity of sight with her. She did not even say goodbye. Nighttime frightens me, when I am alone, or the sounds are unfamiliar.

Morning feels far away. There is some comfort in the notion that Dawn is visiting other shadowed people, whom I have never met, but waited their turn for daybreak too.

Will she remember me? Will my silent longing be loud enough to beckon her back?

Lord, please send me a hand to hold through the night. Touch keeps the blackness at bay.

The Veil

She is looking out the window into her future. What does she see?

What can anyone see of what lies ahead? We play with reading fortune cookies that tell us we will travel or inherit a small fortune. Sometimes we ask for a glimpse, like the trailer for a movie coming out next spring.

At a time in my life when I was slogging through "what is" trying to get to "what will be" I prayed for a sign. I prayed a long time. The reply came like a buoy, and I threw the thin tether of my hopes to it.

"It will be something bigger than you."

What did that even mean? My rescue vessel will be larger than me? It was slim pickings, but it was enough to keep me afloat.

Then it came. It was a female judge behind an imposing desk, looming above my head. Her presence and power felt ominous, and she turned the tide of my life to safer waters.

At another time of desperate petition to God, I begged for a sign that I could actually mother a special needs child.

"He will be carried along on the wave of your family."

Twelve years later, I still hear those words in my head, when our autistic son is thrashing out of control and his brother swoops in to calm him down. The other night I was failing to parent well and texted his sister.

"Want to rescue Ben from me?"

She arrived with fresh energy and took him out for ice cream. When she was beginning to head homeward, he suggested, "We could go to your house, if there's time."

It is exciting to look through the window into tomorrow. But I think there is a good reason for the veil.

Turtle

Some men are like turtles.

There is a protective shell covering the more squishy parts of their anatomy and they have a tendency to hide when company arrives. But I notice that turtles live longer than the more capricious members of the animal kingdom. For example, mayflies flit about like there is no tomorrow, which for them, there isn't.

"Live with abandon," they say. "Leave the ice cream on the counter! Spend the credit cards to the max! Fly in rough neighborhoods!"

Turtles may lead a decidedly more solitary existence but they get more of it (64,000 times more).

I have never heard a clutch of females of any species haranguing tortoises for their reclusive ways, though I will confess I am not fluent in reptilian tongues. Turtles are ok with who they are and no one seems to belittle them or prod them into therapy.

So why are human women discontent with husbands who withdraw into their shells? I know I have wasted a lot of perfectly good adrenaline getting mad at John for sneaking past his adorable family to go play video games. Wordwarp vs. warm blooded children? No contest in my book.

But then some researcher found out that being with people can actually be a stresser for males. (I think he fudged the data to get his own wife to leave him alone with his X-box.) Even John Gray says it's true, and he told me his book has sold more copies than any non fiction title after the Bible. So he must know a thing or two, about marketing if not male tendencies.

John (that's Gray, not Odhner) says it has to do with hormone levels. Two things raise testosterone levels for men: fighting dragons and sitting on the couch. Testosterone reduces stress. If our particular household runs out of dragons, or blown fuses, or mysterious nocturnal noises, John (that's Odhner, not Gray) needs to replenish his supply by doing absolutely nothing, which is camouflaged by sitting in front of an LCD screen with glassy eyes at midnight.

At least I know where to find him, which is more than I can say for the mayfly.

Spaces

I like the spaces in this picture.

The shapes between her hair are like dancing crescent moons, or slices of fleshy white pear.

The space beneath her throat is like an albino trout, sneakily swallowing up her head. Her arms fade into the nothingness around her, like she is part of a dream I am still having.

Even her teeth use up no pixels, compared to the hollow behind them that is dark with the sound of her laughter.

It is easy to heed what takes up ink on a page. It is more challenging to give credence to what is absent.

When I am fretting with the problems that stand in my way like boxwood hedges in a garden maze, it takes effort to observe the emptiness that allows free passage. I may be blind to what is not there, even though it is as real as what is.

Once I was stewing about the hours John was spending at work, when a friend expressed anxiety over her husband's unemployment. Joblessness was a space I had forgotten to notice.

Another time I was sulking about our son's tantrums, when another mother told me her daughter was having daily seizures. I had not considered the absence of that concern in my life.

What are the myriad difficulties that stand like gaping holes in your horizon, because they are not there?

Are they the windows that let you reach the sky?

Darkness Everywhere

I believe there are skylights to heaven.

Darkness can feel like a giant mouth threatening to swallow me up. But then one flashlight, or candle burning is enough to push back the black dragon.

I would be hard pressed to explain to a woman who was born blind precisely what light is like.

"Well, when there is light, you know what is around you and you can find your way, but when the light goes, you can't." I hold my breath as I wait to hear a response.

"Does it happen all at once, this knowing, or bit by bit?" she asks.

"When the light turns on, you can see everything all at once. It is like a whole story in your mind, but then you can pay closer attention and look at this railing, or that wall as if they are sentences and words within the story of the whole building." I wonder if this makes sense.

She shifts her stance, reaching out to trace her fingers along the railing between us. She smiles, perhaps at its hammered surface, maybe imagining this thing I call light.

"I think I would feel safer, knowing where I am and what is

around me. Sometimes the danger of falling and being hurt frightens me." Her smile fades, though she does not seem sad, just longing.

The other day I heard a story about a blackness that is threatening marriage. It hovered over me all day, and I felt chilled in spite of sweaters and sunshine. I stumbled along, not quite seeing my daughters when they chatted to me about the caterpillars that emerged at school. I overheard a brewing tantrum in the other room from Benjamin but it felt too far away. The door swinging open announced that John was walking into the kitchen.

The darkness of what I was stewing about was all around me and I could not see where I was.

Then I looked up and saw John's face. It felt like a skylight to heaven, this man who has been with me through many midnights and numberless dawns. He is God's candle to me, to push the fear back into its shadowy corners, the teeth no longer sharp enough to break my skin.

He smiled and I saw the whole story at once, and it was bright.

Morning Glory

It is astonishing how nourishing a small piece of beauty can be.

One morning glory, which is vastly outnumbered by the man made portion of this New York vista, offers up a dose of loveliness that draws my eyes in and softens my heart. I would wager that you too, gazed first at its azure petals, rather than the dozens of teetering steel steps, hundred or so closed windows, or thousands of sun baked bricks. It does not make sense that a fragile blossom could wield more influence than the towering tenements that surround it to reign in our attention and hold it, like a song amidst the cacophony of traffic.

A lone flower is enough to make this picture worth taking. It will only bloom a short while, though your memory of it can last much longer.

Your marriage has beauty in it, though perhaps it feels overshadowed by a fifty minute commute, or choices that don't open, or thousands of chores lined up like a wall to the sky. Yet the elegance of a simple kindness, offered as unpretentiously as this annual, is enough to make one day worth living. It may only last a short while, but your memory of it can last much longer.

Worn Out

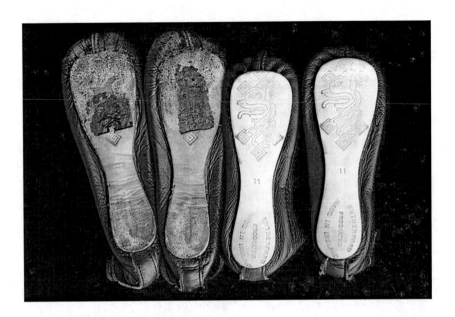

Goodbye is part of the deal.

Unless you can manage to die simultaneously in a car crash, one of you is going to be left behind.

Still, thoughts of widowhood have been safely sequestered away from my consciousness for the past thirty years. But even denial has a saturation point.

I have a cadre of widowed aunts that have bravely shown me what it means to love up until the end and beyond. The messiness of bodies that no longer behave as they were intended took center stage for some of them, while others simply lay in bed next to their husbands whose hands grew quietly cold as they slipped away.

This will never happen to me, of course. At least that is the straw man I hold up against the pounding fear of solitude.

Actually, when the children were small and we had no cell phones, I did think about it. Whenever John was more than an hour late and my imagination went into overdrive, I leaped into a strategic plan of coping as a single mother. I would move in with my parents, thrust my homeschooled children into class-rooms and harness a job. But before I got to the point of taking

John's clothes to Goodwill, he always walked in the door.

Still, all those thoughts were about the children. They never opened the Pandora's box of what it would feel like to be lonely.

The other day John and I went to serenade a widow on her anniversary. She greeted us eagerly, and tearfully put the flowers we offered in a vase as she chatted about her husband of many years. She was bursting with stories and needed tissues as she showed us photographs. I was not feeling particularly nostalgic about John that afternoon, and was carried along by this dear woman's abundant devotion to a man whose hand she could no longer touch.

As we walked out, I thought, "I still have my husband. I could gush a little."

I reached for his hand as we headed home.

Scrabble

My mother adored Scrabble. She devoured cross word puzzles too. Marjorie would tackle the one in the New York Times, carrying it around in her bathrobe pocket, until she had filled in every square. Sometimes she had two going at once. This is probably why her vocabulary left me in the dust with mundane adjectives like cheap, when she was facile with more elegant ones like parsimonious.

Once in a pile of second hand books I found a paperback of crossword puzzles with all the work done for me. Every page had finished riddles on it. If the purpose of such diversions is that the questions are answered, I should have been relieved. What a time saver to buy a book with all the answers already penciled in.

But instead of being thrilled, I was disappointed.

It did not feel as satisfying to just glance at each hard won letter, rather than ferreting them out myself over five mornings of coffee and toast.

I remember wishing that some older person would simply fill in my life's answers for me. Tell me how to respond to an obstreperous three year old. I don't have the time or interest to figure it out. Give me the correct dialogue to employ when conversing with my husband about taxes. I have no need to be innovative, just let me lip sync the right words.

But then it would be no more satisfying than the used paperback.

Fortunately, God is as generous with clues as the editors at the Times. Just let yourself carry the puzzle around in your pocket for a few days or years.

By the way, anyone know an eight letter word for "brisk and cheerful readiness" that has an "a" in the first and third spaces?

Actress

You are a fledgling actress. You are waiting for your first big break when your agent calls to say he landed you an audition in Steven Spielberg's next movie. You are ecstatic! You prepare every way you can think of, and show up on the appointed day. But oh no, there is your competition... Meg Ryan, Julia Roberts, Sandra Bullock and Emma Thompson. You don't stand a chance! Still you give it all you've got, and go home realizing it was a good experience anyway.

The next week your agent calls with the news. You got the

part! It's unbelievable! You tell everyone you know and a bunch that you don't that you have the lead in the next Steven Spielberg movie. You arrive on the set with the excitement exploding inside you. There are hundreds of people there, cameramen, the lighting crew, makeup artists, extras, and then Steven Spielberg saunters over to his director's chair and sits down. There is a hush as he looks at you and nods. Soft music wafts in, the lights turn low. You start your dialogue, gazing at your leading man, passion in your eyes. He says a few lines and then you abruptly yell at the top of your lungs, "CUT!"

Everyone stares at you. The producer's eyebrows go up in alarm, a few jaws slack open. Stephen Spielberg looks over his sunglasses at you as if you have gone crazy.

You start ranting... "This is all wrong.. the music should be more flamboyant, the spotlights need to be on me, I should be in front, not behind this guy..."

Well, that didn't really happen. It will probably never happen. But what does happen on an all too regular basis is that I stand in my living room and yell at my family, "CUT! My husband should be doing more around the house, my kids are too lazy, the house isn't right, the weather is too cold..."

The director of my life's movie is even more qualified than Steven Spielberg.

"Peace has within it confidence that the Lord provides all things, directs all things and leads to an end that is good."
Emanuel Swedenborg

In marriage we have a slight tendency to want to control our partner, to tell them what to say and how to say it, where to be and how to feel. Yet if we really believe the Lord is the director of our life, we will follow His leading, as if He is qualified to do so.

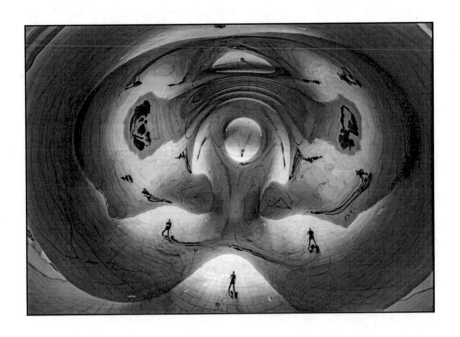

The Only Way Up Is Down

Last night a friend told me six words. *The only way up is down.*

This particular man has earned the prerogative to fling pithy comments at me. I dubbed him "Wise One" last year when he made me laugh and weep and laugh again a fifteen minute trailer about his life.

I immediately thought of a superball, which literally raised the bar for bouncing. The way to get a little neon orb to soar above my head is to slam it to the floor. The friend who coined those six words has himself hit the ground. There are still cement crumbs on his forehead, although his laugh lines provide camouflage.

The four of us were the last lingering guests at the local castle, shooed home by the weary hostess with a key in her hand. We reluctantly ambled to our cars, still clutching the skirts of the evening's Memory even as she strolled up the circular stairs and waved us away. John and I lay our heads in a different state than this couple and last year we lived across an international border, so the time we spend an arm's length from them is in a higher tax bracket than the hours logged filling the dishwasher.

The only way up is down.

The cohesive factor in the invitation list to the night's gala was ordination. These are people for whom wisdom is the quintessential skill on their resume. Yet I have on occasion noticed verbal sparring, not unlike a high school football game, as players scrabbled for the chance to grab the conversation like a football and tear across the field to score a goal of rightness. Wisdom, stripped of humility, loses its patina.

The only way up is down.

As chance would have it the book I am reading reminded me that humility is related to humus, the kind of earth that grows good crops. As a cousin of humility, humus reverberates with the invitation to go down, down on your knees, where the soil is chocolate brown before you stand up and up to reach for a silk tasseled ear of corn high above your heav'n tipped head.

Eat Your Vegetables

It seemed like a good idea at the time. Anyway after we proclaimed it we had to stick with the rule. You know what they say about being consistent. Go ahead and be wrong, but at least do it every time.

The rule was that you had to eat most of your vegetables to get dessert. It sounded like something I had read in a parenting book back when I was still researching the project and not raising actual children.

The glitch was, the vegetable de jour was one of my daughter's most detestables, limas, and she was not biting. This was the obligation between her and an especially decadent lemon meringue pie. I had made it in a binge of domesticity and was dying to see their lip smacking reactions. But I could not slide a slice in front of her until the limas disappeared. I wanted to. Oh, how I wanted to. I offered a compromise.

Half of the pile would suffice. Nope.

How about two spoonfuls? Head shaking.

One bean?

Then I realized. This is how God feels about me.

He has delicious things He wants to give me, if only I will swallow the less appetizing course first. Speaking kindly to my husband when we are late is one lima that comes to mind. Forgiveness when he loses things is another.

"Come on," God coaxes. "Can't you eat just two bites?"

But stubbornness and starvation somehow seem more palatable than a few beans, even with lemony pie in sight.

Being respectful to my spouse is sweeter even than dessert. God cooked up warmheartedness in His kitchen, eagerly anticipating my face as I taste it. I have a hunch it will be worth a plateful of "I am sorry"s and "May I help you look?"s to be served that pièce de résistance.

I will let you know. For now I still have some chewing to do.

Making Tigers

I teach children how to sew. I line up Berninas and Featherweights on the dining room table and arrange rainbow piles of fabric for them to choose from. I try to have every bobbin filled before they arrive, so that the whole ninety minutes is devoted to creating doll clothes and stuffed tigers, not untangling jammed throat plates.

The other day a girl asked for help with her snarled machine and I felt embarrassed at keeping her waiting while I unclogged it. Tugging at lint, I looked over my shoulder at her and noticed not impatience, but curiosity. She seemed as interested in the process of fixing the problem as she was in pinning seams.

I was surprised. This was a novel thought for me. Was it possible that the ability to coax a recalcitrant Singer back into service would benefit her as much as that of gathering a sleeve?

I remembered conversations with women who offhandedly said things like, "I bought an expensive sewing machine, but I cannot get the tension right, so it sits in a closet."

If I empower kids to make pillows and bean bags, but only when I scuttle behind them re-threading and adjusting, have I really launched them? They will be able to create curtains and quilts, but only if the conditions are perfect.

I have heard of couples who have a policy of never arguing in front of the kids. John and I have never been proactive enough to closet our jammed up conversations, and suddenly I wondered if maybe that was a good thing. The kids saw us unpack the feelings, and rephrase the concerns. Maybe those memories will resurface in their minds when their own relationships tangle and snag.

Because every marriage I know of needs a little unclogging once in awhile.

Rapunzel

Those thorns are there for a reason. Beautiful things need to be protected.

I have five daughters. Sometimes the sheer terror of keeping them out of harm's way makes me think that the witch who sequestered Rupunzel was on to something. Rapunzel may have been lonely, but as least she was safe.

Boundaries are one thorn that keeps us from grabbing when we should keep our hands to ourselves. We do well to resist the temptation to tell our partner how he or she feels, or what she or he thinks.

One time John and I were arguing. Vociferously. At one point I shouted, "I am not mad, you are!"

To which he cleverly retorted "I am not angry, YOU are!"

At that point our collective emotional IQ, were it translated to pennies, would not buy a tall latte at Starbucks.

Roses are worth the effort it takes to have a dozen on your coffee table. The scent, when captured in a lead crystal bottle, costs more (Caron Poivre is $1000 per ounce) than the priciest cheese (made from Swedish moose milk, and fetches $500 a pound). The color is lovely enough to be the subject of generations of mushy Valentines, and the velvety petals rival a newborn's fontanel.

Your partner's thoughts are precious too. Maybe that is why some are as hard to get to as Rapunzel. But those timid feelings can be wooed.

I think I will try it.

"John, John, let down your hair."

Outnumbered

There are a lot of reasons to give up.

They stare at me like a mob, ready to become ugly.

Marriage is too much work... we have grown apart... I am exhausted from trying to be understood... the kids take all my energy... he is not the man I thought he was... everyone else has a better marriage than this... we were too young when we started... he works too many hours... we don't have enough money... I need time for me...

Their chants grow louder between my ears and I get smaller with each pulsing accusation.

But then I silence them all with one sweep of my outstretched hand.

Eyes still gaping, they are suddenly frozen and mute.

In the calming quiet, I see that they are only pretend. They are all made of plastic.

"I promised to love him always!" I say with a strength that surprises even me.

Then a great hand reaches from above and scoops them all away.

Wizard of Oz

The kids were watching the Wizard of Oz in the same room where I was sewing. Having watched it umpteen times over my lifetime I could listen over my shoulder and picture the images easily.

The bumblebee music.... Miss Gulch on her bicycle.

Squeaky voices... Munchkin land.

Thundering threats... Toto is pulling back the curtain.

What surprised me though was how quickly everything whizzed by. My memory was much more e-l-o-n-g-a-t-e-d. The days Dorothy spent wistfully singing about a rainbow wishing someone would listen to her clicked by in a trice. The whirling tornado was gone before I could finish two seams. The flying monkey scene lasted eighty seconds.

It smacked up against my sense of time. When I am slogging through a painful ordeal, it feels like six o'clock traffic in Manhattan. Nothing could be slower. If I dredge up the excruciating events in my memory banks... I can with effort remember that they felt strung out. But looking back they are diluted by other emotions. At the risk of minimizing my own suffering I hear myself mollifying an earlier me.

"Three kids in cloth diapers? Meh."

"Twelve hospitals for Benjamin before he was three? Not so bad."

"Driving with six kids across the country in a decrepit car? We made it."

Yet the frightening parts are crucial to the story. If Dorothy's house had not begun to pitch, the Wicked Witch of the West hadn't written her name in the sky, and the poppies had not lulled them to sleep she would never have discovered her own resilience. Frank Baum could have saved a lot of ink by having Dorothy realize in the opening scene that there's no place like home.

I guess God could save a heap of trouble too by telling me on my second birthday what it is taking me a lifetime to figure out. But the Dorothy who clicked her heels three times was a different girl than the one who fell into the pig pen. And I hope that the wife and mother I am becoming looks like a color version of the sepia me.

Help

Dear Lord,

Why do I think I can do it without you? Why would I WANT to do it without you? My toddlers had not the slightest hesitation to ask for help, every day, many times a day, and I gave it willingly much of the time. Am I a more loving parent than You? Hardly.

On the Other Side of Won't

One of my tendencies is to agree to do things. I offer, or people ask me about a volunteer opportunity down the road and my knee jerk response is "Sure!"

Then as the time to show up looms closer my shoulders drop and I shake my head.

"Why did I agree to give away a whole Saturday morning?"

But there is a rubber band inside me, one end latched on the promise I made last month and the other to my leaden feet. It helps to accelerate my reluctant self and yank me through unwillingness.

Last Saturday was one of those days. I had cheerfully consented to babysit the kids who showed up for an event at church. I like kids. But the day before the event the number of children coming mushroomed from five with no boys or babies to fourteen with boys and babies.

Now let me hasten to assure you that I love boys. I have taken them to the stream to catch crayfish, and watched their delight over marshmallow shooters, seen their tousled heads tucked over a box of Legos fishing for the little man piece and helped them build forts out of sticks and cardboard. I also am a long time baby lover. A single innocent baby can stop my grumpiness in its tracks with one eye open. But boys and babies take a different strain of attention than five little girls chatting over crayons, and did I mention that the time commitment was 4 1/2 hours?

So I drove to the event with John, while he listened to my complaints. Being a wise man, he made no comment that could possibly be gnarled into ammunition for my rant. He said guarded things like, "I love you."

But as each sunny child came around the corner and joined us at a table full of play dough, my annoyance evaporated. Three middle school girls came to my rescue and raised the big person/little person ratio. It was a very enjoyable morning. We did not hunt crayfish but we did shoot marshmallows.

I think God knows this about me. Perhaps He knows it about you. He gets us to say yes to marriage when our belly is full and our heart is resplendent. He attaches the thick rubber band of commitment here. Then comes the middle of the story when saying yes does not feel like a brainy idea anymore.

I sometimes listen to couples on the other side of here. These are the ones who have flung through tougher stuff than I could have predicted based on research in songs by the Beach Boys or movies like *Anne of Green Gables*. These couples have been stretched like a brown rubber band, to love each other across messy terrain, to hang on tight when the speed picked up.

But would I really elect to have missed the wiz bang of a ride to stay where I was when I began?

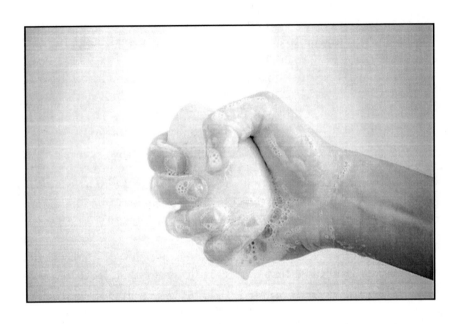

Washable

I love that people are washable.

There have been times that my children or I were so covered in unmentionable substances I threw away the clothes we were wearing. But the bodies.... oh the bodies are incredibly resilient. Even the permanent marker tatoos toddlers gave themselves eroded eventually, and I might add disappeared more quickly than the unauthorized hair cuts did.

One of the healing messages I kept close from my Aunt Louise was that "I have feelings, but I am not my feelings. I have thoughts, but I am not my thoughts."

This has been a freeing truth, when I find myself covered in grimy emotions and notions.

Once I was angry at John for some infraction. I was driving with him to get the car worked on, figuring out how to cram this annoying errand in between time sensitive obligations. Then he said that he had checked on line and there was a movie theater across from the mechanic, playing the movie I had been wanting to see, and would end just a little late for me to get to work, but he would cover for me until I got there. Would I like to go enjoy a movie?

The anger was transported to someplace in another hemisphere, and in the vacuum, came gratitude.

I am not my feelings. I may let them glom onto me, but I can banish them. Remembrance of why I love my husband is a good deterrent. I have even been known to keep a list of anti resentment protection in my pocket.

Fallen Leaves

I drive the same road four times every day. The canopy of leaves spreads over me, waving as I go by. Their colors do not change noticeably from April to August but when the first chills of autumn blow through, they are transformed. I say transformed as if it happens in a blink, but actually the shift is subtle enough to ignore it if you have a mind to. It is not hard to stay riveted to the newscaster, or my ipod, or the annoyingly careful driver in front of me. The trees never actually cry out "Look at me! I am different!". It takes attention to appreciate.

At first I wonder if it has actually begun. There are edges of red on the branches, but maybe they were there yesterday. That tree bending over the stone wall seems more yellow than last week, or maybe even this morning. After a few days of the palette sliding from cool green to warm scarlet and gold, I start to feel as if I too want to change. What is it like to see new hues spreading across your arms, a response to an invisible clarion call? What does the reckless abandon of letting everything that appears to protect and cover you fall away feel like? Do the trees fully realize that this explosion of color is the last gasp of life from leaves whose journey will carry them to the mulchy ground, and a crunchy, brown grave?

There was a period when the way my husband and I handled expenses was driving a wedge in our relationship. The more I gritted my teeth and insisted he keep better records and submit receipts, the chillier our financial exchanges became. I had known years ago that money was not the driving force of how he operated, and that seemed very quaint and endearing at the time. Now it was maddening.

Then I began to see things, well differently. It was subtle at first, rather like the first amber tips of the sycamores that cover my head in September. I thought, "Well I could keep those records. I could pay the bills."

It meant that part of me had to die. My rightness, and need to cling to "the principle of the thing" had to take on new colors, like the deep red of acceptance, and the orange of mutual trust. We might even lose money in the process, if the transition was choppy. Little deaths, of having things my way, or controlling my husband fell to my feet and became the compost for compassion, and patience.

But what of the spring? I am old enough to know that all that stands between these piles of decaying leaves and miniature green shoots that appear from nowhere is about a hundred sunrises. Three full moons, give or take a little. Could the distance between the complaining me and the peaceful one be so short? But what I really want to know and am afraid to ask is, Can I get to the new life without actually having to die?

"He that finds his life will lose it, and he that loses his life for my sake will find it."
Matthew 10:39

I guess not.

But why would I cling to something lifeless anyway? Criticism and resentment are as dead as the fallen leaves. Would I really like to somehow fasten them back to my fingers and use them to beautify myself? Waiting for tiny signs of kindness in the spring seems like an improvement on the old me. Recently my husband made a mistake, and I didn't feel an irresistible urge to point it out to him. It's subtle. But I think I will let the leaves lie where they fall.

Listening

Yeats says that "To understand is to love."

I know it feels incredibly good to toss a feeling to John, and have him catch it. Sometimes it is spoken, other times it is in a glance, like last night. Benjamin was trying to apologize to me for his angry outburst, and he actually folded his hands and asked me to please, please forgive him. He did not go down on his knees, but it sure reminded me of the apology Anne Shirley made to Rachel Lynde in Anne of Green Gables. The humorous part for me, was that although Anne was saturated in drama... Benjamin meant it from the bottom of his heart. Looking over his little penitent head at John and bouncing smiles between us made the whole scene worth the wear and tear on my nerves. Don't tell Benjamin though. It may not work twice.

Having someone who listens is one of the blessings marriage is designed to include. We don't always manage to figure out how, but it is what God had in mind when He invented it.

I suppose if we were better studies in the art of full attention, we would slide to the top of the Marital Success Scale and we could all go home. But most of us find ways to complicate something that is actually pretty simple.

Look at this series of photographs.

1.One girl talks and the other listens.
2.The second girl talks and her sister listens.
3.They both feel good.

How is it that people with advanced degrees and triple digit IQ's have trouble with this?

Fortunately we get lots of chances to get it right. 365 per year on average, unless you spend part of every year in solitary confinement.

And as Anne also said, "Today is fresh, with no mistakes yet."

Try to listen to the person you love as if you want to understand. You will both feel good.

Bleeding Heart

Mine is a bleeding heart. Why must there be blood to be alive? Why the endless pumping, going in circles, carrying, nourishing, taking out the exhausted byproducts of living? Why the vulnerability, that shows up every time I am wounded? More blood, more of my limited love supplies, spilled and spent.

Marriage asks so much of me. It asks me to give today, last week, and more than likely tomorrow too.

Yet, like the flower that appears in my garden on a spring day, the love I give and give and give again was not really mine to begin with. It showed up, boon of my bones, when some unknown force knew I was in short supply. Come to think of it, it shows up every time I need it, no matter how much gets spilled.

Thank you, Lord, for the bleeding heart.

Emerging

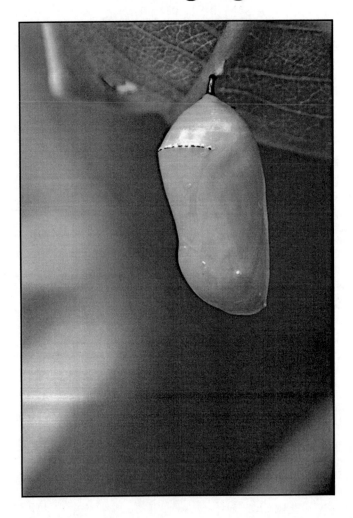

Recently the world turned its attention to the rescue efforts in Chile. Thirty three men were trapped in the bowels of the earth for two months, while hundreds if not thousands of people combined efforts and resources to lift them back to the surface in a cramped capsule.

I have not a clue how much the rescue cost in terms of dollars and pesos, but I suspect generosity won the day. I can only imagine the animated meetings of engineers, miners, geologists and medical consultants as they predicted and implemented their plans to save the lives of men they had never met. It is possible that members of the rescue team had in the past year crossed paths with some of the trapped men on the streets of San Jose, and felt not a trace of interest in their difficulties. But in the scenario of the collapsed mine, these victims sprang to the limelight and captured our global compassion.

While I join the universal sentiment of wishing these men well, whose names and pasts held not a whit of bearing on their worth as salvable, I am jealous.

Why is it that three dozen persons who are separated from their families by tons of rock are supremely deserving of the collective endeavor of a nation, while numberless men are separated from their families through divorce every day of every year on every corner of the globe?

For one thing, no one wasted any time asking if the people wanted to get out.

"Perhaps they chose to escape their problems. We should not force them to come back if they don't want to," was not a quote I heard from any CNN reporters.

It is not so safe talking about a return from pending divorce. People get feisty, when you start exploring ways to reconcile. There is a taboo around reaching out to people whose lives are caving in.

The other day I hugged a friend whose sibling is experiencing a marital conflict. I tried to express empathy for her pain in watching a family she loves suffer. She said I was the first person to acknowledge her hurt.

Is that possible? I suspect that complete strangers will be contacting the wives of the miners for the near future, saying, "I saw you on tv! I am so sorry for your ordeal and happy for your husband's safe return!"

Yet my friend passes people she has known for years in a code of silence?

No one would say that getting the men through the shaft was easy, or cheap. Perhaps bringing husbands and wives back together means moving heaven and earth too.

The part that breaks my heart is how skittish we are about trying.

Intensive Italian

My daughter Hosanna is taking Intensive Italian. I have offered several times to help her study but she has not taken me up on it.

Instead Hosanna's professor connected her to a college student in Milano who wants to practice her English. The two girls skype for an hour or so each week, and Hosanna says her fluency is molta migliore. As a sophomore at a brainy women's college, she has to jam the commitment in between Multivariable Calculus and Mathematical Methods in Physical Sciences. But she wants to do well, and so she chooses to show up, every week.

It is a win win situation, really. Not only are they getting to know each other, both girls are expanding their view of the world, Hosanna's GPA is going up and they are si divertono..

This is what marriage mentoring looks like, too. A younger couple goes out with more experienced couple and they talk for an hour or so each month. They get to know each other, they expand their views of il matrimonio, the younger couple raises their MPA and they have il divertimento.

In a world where lots of efforts at marital improvement carry a hefty sticker price, mentoring is low budget: the price of due tazze di caffe, and a commitment to show up.

It will probably give you more l'amore, too.

Irresistible

It looks like it is easy to love this baby. She doesn't have to keep up her end of the conversation, or do anything fascinating, or offer to chip in for her share of lunch for people around her to think she is scrumptious company. Even introverted adults will stretch their facial muscles, emit purring sounds and play peek a boo to coax a smile from a nine month old. Outlandish behaviors like puking are routinely overlooked.

I have witnessed professional businessmen in three piece suits peel off all reticence when their baby enters the room. A minute earlier they were speaking to clients in sentences with four syllable adjectives and prepositional phrases, but as soon as their infant appears they are reduced to high pitched baby talk.

It is an interesting contrast, how little babies have to perform for how much we adore them.

Why do we love them?

This woman with the scrunched up face is approximately 64 times as old as the baby she wants to impress. That much distance enables her to be lavish with forgiveness of minor transgressions like an inability to walk, or low performance in academics. If I ask her why she thinks this baby is irresistible, her response is likely to be vague. I don't think the reaction even travels through her frontal cortex, but simply goes from her heart to her mouth.

I remember times when I was bleary eyed from lack of continuous sleep, carrying my twins into the store, and a complete stranger would interrupt my errand to pour attention on the girls. Often, someone would simply want to touch their fuzzy heads. He would explain that his sisters were twins, or he was a twin, or his second cousin's niece's next door neighbor just had twins....and I would be yanked back from exhaustion into the reality that these little girls are incredibly precious. Thank you, stranger, for the wake up call.

Your spouse, present or future, is somebody's baby. He or she is lovable and worthy of kisses, regardless of any ability to keep up the conversation or pay for lunch. Angels, the ones whose perspective is blessed by more longevity than mine, are more lavish with forgiveness of mistakes than I sometimes manage to be. If I could find a way to ask them why they think my husband is so cute, I have a feeling the answer would be vague.

Sometimes in the midst of mundane life with John, I try to squint my eyes and look for the angels, hovering around him in complete devotion. I picture them trying to coax a smile from him on a hard day, eager to soften his worries, perhaps just wanting to touch him.

I wonder if they want me to help.

"Angels observe what is good in other people, and if they see anything evil and false, they excuse it, and if they can, try to amend it in them. They use all their might to excuse it and put a good interpretation on their actions."
Emanuel Swedenborg, *Secrets of Heaven* 1079

Graffiti

I have always been repulsed by graffiti. Brazen boys in LA would scale barbed fences and climb twenty feet above the concrete to spray paint a cocky message above the 405 Freeway. I was not impressed by their bravado. I was annoyed. Who were they to trash the road sides, the trees and the public bathrooms? The miscreants have an ongoing tussle with maintenance departments, who roll in with their state funded trucks to eradicate the swirling script.

There are names and dates splattered across the cabins in the western Pennsylvania woods we have slept in for two decades. I began to think of them as people, not just pen names. Did Josie and Billy ever come back, curious to see if their clandestine mark was still visible twenty years later?

Misdemeanors aside, I wonder what urgings bubble out in the form of painted fonts and scribbled watermarks. Are the paintbrushes fueled by a lonely teenagers who crave to be visible? Do the authors hunger for someone, even a stranger, to be a witness to their words?

Marriage is intended as a place where two people are heard deeply, seen sincerely. It takes a lifetime to learn how to listen to the meaning disguised by patter and to look for the splendor wrapped in the mundane.

I wonder if the maintenance crews could be made obsolete by families that know what it means to be fully present with each other.

Scuba Diving

Tim and Rhonda loved to go scuba diving. They had explored caves in the Cayman Islands, Indonesia and Baja. The underwater world drew them to its silent depths with a pull like the invisible ocean currents that carry orcas to the Canadian coast.

They had invested in premier equipment over the years, Nova fins and frameless masks. The sport had become more than a shared interest. It had mushroomed to a passion.

One time Rhonda was diving with a less experienced diver, while Tim was on the boat with a group of friends enjoying the cerulean water.

Tim began to expect his wife to appear on the surface, and watched for the break in the water as she pulled off her snorkel and threw back the whip of her wet hair. But none came. The clock said that her tanks were more empty than full and anxiety was filling the space in his own lungs.

Abruptly Tim yanked on his gear and plunged into the water. He sank quickly to the mouth of the cave Rhonda was exploring and slipped into the opening, which was no wider than a couch cushion.

Within a few interminable minutes Tim saw Rhonda and her partner, behind a looming boulder. He swam to them and motioned feverishly to them to follow. He pulled them both to the door of the cave and tugged them to the surface.

The friends on the boat caught the sense of urgency and helped lift the two exhausted divers into the boat.

"What happened?" Tim's voice was laced with fear and anger that his wife had been reckless.

Rhonda was groggy, and slumped into his arms. Tim would have to wait for an explanation. That night, after food and water, Rhonda told the story of how they had been lured by a school of fish deeper into the cave and had lost their bearings. The meter on the tank said that they had plenty of time, and they kept exploring. But they were becoming confused, and neither of them knew the way back. Tim had put away Rhonda's tank and seen the malfunctioning meter. It misled them. He held her tightly and swung up a prayer of thanks that she was safe.

Years later, Tim and Rhonda were more consumed by jobs and children than diving. His work week seeped into the evenings and weekends, and she was involved in the many aspects of their three children's lives. She had forgotten to wait for his homecoming each night, because it was so erratic. They got sloppy about knowing where each other was, and whether they were safe.

Tim was spending his best hours with a female coworker, going out to lunch, and feeling successful about their shared projects. He enjoyed their time together.

Then one Saturday when Rhonda was straightening the garage, she unearthed their scuba equipment. Holding the tank that had once deceived her into lingering within the darkness of the cave, her memories rose to the surface. Wrapped around the images came a piercing message.

"Go find Tim. He is running out of air."

Startled, Rhonda felt a rushing sense of urgency. How had she not noticed? Tim was gone more than he was home, and seemed lured into a relationship with a coworker. Who was she?

Rhonda leaped into her car and sped to Tim's office. Her heart raced as she heard the pieces that she had dismissed click together. Taking two steps at a time Rhonda flung through the door to see her husband sitting on the couch with his arm around a woman she did not know.

Tim leaped to his feet and the other woman yanked at her skirt.

"Rhonda, what are you doing here?" he stammered.

"What happened?" Rhonda's voice was laced with fear and anger that her husband had been reckless.

"Come with me. Now." Rhonda was shaking.

They drove home, with terse dialogue piercing the silence.

Tim was confused, and defensive. He had not fully realized where he was drifting to.

Rhonda wept. Tim shuddered at his own blatant foolishness. They untangled the darkness that had curled its fingers around their marriage.

Rhonda held him tightly, hurling up a prayer of thanks that he was safe.

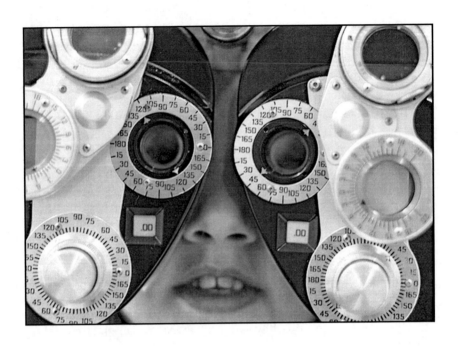

Eye Exam

Going to the eye doctor makes me a little anxious.
"Is this better? Or this? This one, or this?"
The questions come quickly along with the clicking.
I want to give the right answer, really I do. But it all happens so fast. I know he is trying to fit me for the very best glasses, but I still have the sinking feeling that the doctor will abruptly say, "You jerk. You are wrong. This one is not better!"

My cousin once showed me something I have never forgotten. She laid a pair of forks on the table and asked me to choose the best one.

I stared. I looked for clues. I worried. I think my blood pressure went up. Probably my cholesterol too. Then, tentatively, I picked one, poised for her to shout, "Right!" or "Wrong!" I felt no joy, only uncertainty that I had picked the wrong one.

Then she laid a pair of spoons down. She picked one up and gave it to me. I looked at her face. I said "Thank you," as she placed it in my hand. I smiled. She smiled. I felt grateful for the spoon.

Such a simple gesture, really. But it showed me the difference between a gift and the pressure of picking for myself. All right, all right, calm down. I am not saying that we should never choose for ourselves. But I am curious about the different ways those processes feel.

Unless you live in Bombay, you probably picked your own spouse. Perhaps there was some anxiety around the choosing, using up gobs of air time as you analyzed his personality with twenty seven personal dating coaches for potential character unbalances. Maybe it was as instantaneous as the scene in "Sleepless in Seattle" where she hears him on the radio and just knows.

But in either case, God has given this person to you to love and respect... today. You can stare, and look for clues that he is really the right one. You can second guess your decision, worry, and feel your blood pressure rise. You may ask disillusioned girlfriends " Did I marry the wrong guy?"

Or you can open your eyes each morning, look into his unwashed face, smile, and say "Thank you for marrying me."

My Foot Hurts

I twisted my ankle a few weeks ago. There were no athletic feats involved, just a pair of Danskos and an uneven surface. I wrapped it in a bandage and wobbled along on crutches for a few days, but mostly it was just weak and tender.

I resisted using the crutches as it was a magnet for attention. I did not want to divert compassion from people who actually deserve it, like the boy who recently had brain surgery, or the woman whose sister died. I preferred to limp along, propping the whole leg up when I could. If it was convenient to not mention it, I didn't. But I was reluctant to do extra walking. When I was at a friend's house five doors away, I asked her to drive me home, even though I looked pretty lazy.

One thing I noticed was a sharp increase in my protective body space. If anyone or anything came within eighteen inches of the ankle my hackles went up, and I activated an invisible force field. Even small smacks from chairs or limbs reverberated the pain. This was a shift from my regular stance. After nine children and twenty five years of breastfeeding I ordinarily have no residual response to being sat on or yanked. Other people's babies can grab my hair and plant an applesaucey fist on my shoulder and I don't flinch.

But for a few weeks I sent out the subliminal message. Don't mess with my ankle.

Recently I was commiserating with a friend about why our husbands avoid talking about feelings. It looks easy enough to me. I could even provide multiple choice.

1. I am mad at you.
2. I am not mad at you.
3. Leave me alone while I figure out whether I am mad at you.
4. Give me ten reasons not to be mad at you.

But instead they emit an electrical charge like the ones that keep beagles in the yard. Stay back.

This is perplexing. I am tempted to call him lazy. Is it really so dangerous? Or are they reacting from a pain that I cannot see and perhaps did not create?

John can tell you the physiology of how men's reaction to shame occurs in the same part of their brain that responds to pain. He understands this. I almost do too. But it does not unfetter him from the discomfort. And he would prefer not to mention it.

Legacy

Zachary's lacrosse coach is the son of my long time friends. The other day I was watching a game and the coach greeted another spectator with an enthusiastic hand shake and a smile. The small gesture made me inhale sharply. In that split second he looked exactly like his father, a man of integrity. In fact he reminded me of his grandfather as well. I felt a surge of fondness for all three men and the not so invisible threads between them.

It is not news that children look and behave like their parents. Cleft chins, wide noses and distinctive gaits show up years later in the faces and legs of people who are oblivious to the obvious. Sometimes I look at my own sons and marvel at the resemblance to the man I chose to love. Is it genetic? Is it contagion?

Of course it is not only the sterling attributes that are carried on. My girls are laissez-faire about picking up their paraphernalia and I do not need to wonder where that comes from. Although I never made any pronoucements about the right way to toss off shoes when you come in the door, my kids have eyes. They followed suit.

Children learn the ways of relationships from their parents too. John and I cringe to remember the lessons we passed on to our older kids about yelling. We may never have declared it as an effective tool for communication but we certainly demonstrated it as the method of choice. Two decades later we have changed. Yelling is an anomaly in our home now. It happens but certainly not every day and sometimes not even every week. I believe that this impacts the last of our kids in ways that will bear fruit for them and even for their children.

I suppose if I had realized in those early years that the echo of my screeching would reverberate for half a century I might have clenched my teeth a little harder.

Spell Check

Spelling is easier than it used to be.

Not because the occurrences of obstreperous spellings have diminished, but because of the handy little red line that appears when we make a mistake. I appreciate that there is no penalty for trying, and even repeated failures. It is different with my ATM card, that yells at me when I mess up three times and snatches my card away. Probably the teller that gets minimum wage for screening hours of mundane interactions gets a good laugh and tells his friends about the lame lady who cannot remember her PIN. That happened to me in Paris. I cringe to think of them mocking me in French.

But with computers you have a nonjudgemental advocate hiding beneath the keys who nonchalantly brings small errors to your attention immediately, so you can actually redeem yourself before you click on send or worse yet, print.

You are not an unprecedented jerk. You simply cannot figure out the minutiae of vowels and prefixes that take inordinate delight in fooling us. Hence the handiness of the spell checker.

A couple we know came up with a similar scheme for routine inter-relational mistakes.

"ouch."

It does not even get a capital letter because it is supposed to be said surreptitiously, not announced.

When one of you says something that causes the other discomfort, the appropriate response is "ouch." It does not heap shame and revenge on the speaker, it simply underlines the words, giving one a chance to amend them.

I am grateful for the spell checker that redirected me approximately seventeen times in this short diatribe, perhaps convincing you that I can indeed spell proficiently.

I am equally grateful to John, who quietly gives me another opportunity to speak kindly.

Sickness

Once upon a time there was a little girl named Martha with wispy blond hair and blue eyes. Her parents loved her dearly and rejoiced in her sweet nature. They bought her dolls and books, a teddy bear and beautiful dresses. She made fairy houses in the back yard, and had picnics under the table on rainy days. Martha wore her mother's white dress for pretend weddings, a bunch of violets clutched in her hand. Their family was very happy.

But when Martha was eight, she started to feel sluggish. Her parents wondered about it, and tried to feed her extra spinach, but it never occurred to them to take her to a doctor. They felt reticent about exposing their difficulties to a complete stranger, and did not really believe he could help anyway. Their daughter was sick, and that was that.

Over the next few months Martha had a steady decline. She laughed less. She stayed in bed rather than played outdoors in the sunshine. She lost weight, and her cheeks were wan. The light in her eyes faded to a dull and listless gaze.

The parents were increasingly worried, but they tried to hide the problem. When children invited Martha over they made excuses, without admitting that she was too exhausted to come.

Martha's grandparents began to ask poignant questions, but the parents were evasive and private about the problem. They felt isolated, and deeply ashamed that they were failing to care for their precious daughter.

Martha died of leukemia a week before her tenth birthday. She closed her blue eyes on a stormy winter night and never opened them again.

The condition she had was completely curable.

Couples whose marriages are sick are often skittish about seeking help. A friend of ours did a study of why couples wait until the marriage is all but lifeless to finally go for counseling. The reasons they gave were vague.

If parents want to give the best to their child, including warm clothes and good health care, an intact family should be at the top of the list.

Many of the maladies that claim marriages are completely curable.

Expiration Date

Yesterday I pulled out a jar of vitamins. The expiration date was November 2006. I wondered whether the nutritional punch was still held captive in the bottle or had leaked into the cupboard, fortifying the pressed board over the last six years.

I tossed them.

Last week I tried to make room in the fridge for our new boarders. I extracted salad dressings, mayo and mustard that were fourteen years old... in dog time. Why would I smear old condiments on crisp lettuce or fragrant whole wheat?

Crusty items seem to hang around way past their prime, cluttering the space I should keep clear for tastier fare. Why is it hard to let go? They no longer serve us.

A dear uncle in his eighties and I were chatting recently. He could not remember the details of what he wanted to tell me, and felt embarrassed. I sometimes wonder if the forgetfulness of old age is actually a blessing. Some of the clutter in our brains is outdated too. Do we really need to be concerned with our second cousin's neighbor's daughter's dog? The absence of such trivia makes airy room for the more current and genteel concerns of the wise.

A friend mentioned that her husband no longer speaks with his brother. It is especially painful because the brother has cancer, and they cannot cross the breach between them. I asked what began the disconnect.

"Nine years ago my husband stopped in for an impromptu visit when he was driving through. It was a bad time and he never forgave him."

Really? One misunderstanding obliterates forty years of brotherhood? It was time to chuck that grudge in the trash.

Hearing this travesty turned a spotlight on my own archaic responses to hurts from the last millennium. Even the IRS obeys a three year statute of limitations. Do I want to be more vindictive than them?

I admitted to myself that I am harboring resentment about a choice John made in 1992. Get a grip, woman. If there is a saturation point for my brain do I actually want to waste precious shelf space with moldy memories?

Happiness Plan

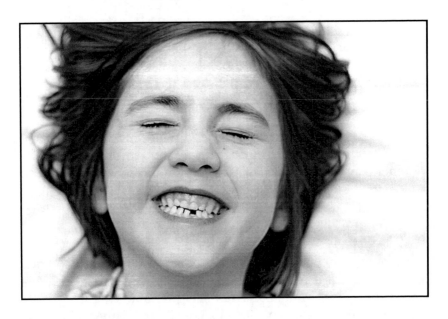

I need to begin with a disclaimer. I am not partial to making my own personal happiness the guiding star of my decisions. But the article my sister sent me about 12 Things Happy People Do Differently did strike a chord or two. In fact it set off the whole xylophone. While setting out to please myself does not make a good launching pad it can be helpful to take cues from people who have figured out how to participate with The Happiness Plan. God wants us to be happy, of that I am sure. After all I am only a proxy parent, and I rush into burning buildings, scale barbed wire with bleeding palms and grind wheat to bake bread for my children on a daily basis. Could I expect less from the Divine?

The list includes appreciation, forgiveness, optimism, and nourishing relationships. It elaborates about savoring life's blessings, making a commitment, practicing spirituality and kindness. These choices, claim the authors, are descriptive of happy people. I am especially glad to hear the promo for commitment. I am a fan of commitment.

Actually the closer I look, the more congruence I find with their list and my composite picture of God. He is the Dayspring of kindness, even when we hijack the credit for ourselves. He invented forgiveness to help us find our way home. When we pound forgiveness into our muscle memory as well it brightens the path.

The God of Appreciation chose to saturate the world with ways to affirm His children. Gratitude is the matrix within which people can thrive. Fortunately we are surrounded by potential appreciaters. When each of us figures out the Secret and starts dishing out thanks for the abundance in which we are all swimming, everyone wins.

The authors point to optimism as a signature characteristic of joy. I believe that God cannot even frown on us. That is optimism in the extreme.

For my final thesis in college I asked 300 children to describe God on a 3x5 index card. I saved my favorites, including one from a little girl named Katie.

"HY IS OWESE HAPPEE"

I guess I will make God the guiding star of my decisions, and let Him work out the details about happiness.

Compost

I had a friend named Carol who was a committed gardener. Vegetables flourished under her touch and flowers bordered her yard. One day we were eating with our kids at the park, chatting while they played out of hearing but not out of sight. She finished a banana and slipped the peel into her bag.

"Why don't you just throw it away?" I asked in my ignorance.

"I save all my compost," she laughed.

To me, an empty peel was trash to be tossed at the first receptacle. But to Carol it was food for tomatoes that she had not even planted yet. Compost takes months to ripen. She was banking on the assurance that she would still be gardening a year from now.

For a long time I had a strategy for unwanted criticisms. I tossed them. They were garbage, not worth my time. But more recently I have been trying to hold them as if they can fertilize me. Often I realize that the lesson is too late for the current faux pau, but that chances are high that I will stumble into the same mistake next month.

The other day a woman blew me off. I was talking about something precious to me and she hijacked the conversation and went in her own direction. I was bruised, feeling as if I had held out my throbbing heart and she carelessly pushed it aside. But I used it for compost. I resolved to work harder not to do that to anyone else. I now knew more vividly what dismissal looked like.

Marriage is a do-si-do of infractions. If my partner forgets to clear his things from the dining room table I can tuck the memory in my pocket for when my sewing project is sprawled all over the floor. If I feel jilted that he does not ask about my day I can use the sting to motivate me to ask about his.

It is a blessing really, to bump up against someone who can help me learn from my mistakes. Because I plan on being in this marriage 100 years from now.

Monotonous

I bought a ticket for Marital Bliss a long time ago, and boarded the train. It has been a tedious trip already and we are not there yet. Sometimes the scenery is incredible... lush with fields of wildflowers and open skies.

Today though, the view outside my window is blahh. The sky is gray, and the air pricks at my hands until I pull on my gloves. It looks less like the glossy pamphlets I saw when I chose this destination and more like the forgotten part of town.

Frankly, I am sick of the journey. How long is this supposed to take anyway? I did not actually check the arrival time when I bought my ticket, but I sure wasn't expecting this. I started out happy, I want to get to happy, so why this protracted detour?

It is not as if I am bleeding or in pain. It just feels monotonous sometimes... well most of the time. I go to bed with all the dishes done and the counter wiped clean, and by the time kids whoosh off to school it is littered with last night's cereal and ice cream bowls, and this morning's hurried juice glasses. Can't we all try fasting?

John and I connect occasionally, but there is hubbub in between when I have no idea what he is thinking and he certainly does not know how I am feeling.

It reminds me of a hem stitch. You do not want thread to show on the front of the garment, so you travel along on the back for half an inch, take a tiny stitch, another long hidden stretch, a tiny stitch, all the way around the circumference of the dress. It does hold the hem, so I guess it works for the girl wearing it. Can our sporadic attachment hold us together while we wear this marriage?

I can hear the chugging of the train, underneath my own grumbling, so I suppose we are getting somewhere. But the sense of progress is hard to detect. I wish the conductor would stroll through the aisle every few hours, and announce that we are indeed fifty or a hundred miles closer to Marital Bliss.

"Next stop, Marital Bliss. Marital Bliss, comin' up next,"

I guess I need to trust the tireless commitment of the Engineer.

Higgs Bosen

My daughter traded cars with us last weekend so that her dad would have a chance to take hers to the mechanic. She called today to ask me if it was fixed yet. I paused.

"Sorry. It is still in the driveway."

"I love Dad," she said with a sigh. There was no residual sarcasm, or ridicule in her voice. She was just reminding herself that she loves him, in a dimension that cannot be flattened by his tendency to forget things.

Yesterday he called her just to share his excitement about the biggest triumph in physics in fifty years. Hosanna's degree is in physics, so he felt she would understand in a way I did not. He had tried to impart the magnitude of the discovery to me but I confess my enthusiasm was plastic.

"Great. A new particle. We didn't have quite enough, I guess," I sounded like my kids do when I say we are having stir fry for dinner. He held his tongue about my inability to absorb the magnitude of the situation.

I was touched by her knee jerk response about the car. I doubt whether those are the first three words to spring from my lips when John does not do what I asked.

My deer tick sized understanding of the Higgs boson is that this particle is the one that holds all the others together. Scientists knew it was there, but they could not find it. It is the magic ingredient for mass, gravity and inertia. Without it we would dissipate, lacking any pull toward each other. We would be unable to keep going.

It reminds me of another magical element... the one Hosanna managed to find even in the gap between what she had asked for and what she got.

Unresolved Chord

I was listening to a piece of music this morning. I don't know the composer, but the ending is still with me. There was a chord that leaned like a Lamborghini tilted on its right wheels, going around the corner in a Steve McQueen car chase. It begged for resolution. The song finally slid into the dominant and my shoulders uncurled.

Probably there is a mathematical equation producers use to stretch out a dramatic scene so that it sends a jolt of adrenaline surging through the audience like a zap of electricity without actually frying them. Since I watch fewer movies than most people I have a lower threshold. My kids often stop watching the movie and start watching me as I spring from my seat in panic.

No doubt there is a secret formula for musicians too, as they compose a fugue or a twangy love song. An augmented seventh wakes up a somnolent listener, raising their eyebrows for the finale.

John loves barbershop tunes, which typically fling the last few notes of the tagline like kids at Disneyland who refuse to "keep their arms and legs inside the car until it comes to a full and complete stop".

The other day I was at a party and noticed the dissonance playing out in many of the lives around me.... relationships that teetered on two wheels, health issues pending resolution, jobs going over the cliff, marriages headed for a crash.

Although I hesitate to compare God to the likes of Robert Wagner, they both seem to employ a theme of tension. Yet in the case of God, resolution comes flooding in like a full orchestra.

My mother's final years had more discord than the michelins at an Indy 500. She had been separated from her husband for the last ten years of his life. Then she was widowed for ten more. Mom lost everything she owned in a flood, then watched the replacements float away in a second deluge. Her vision succumbed to cataracts, her strength to anemia. One nurse in the hospital when she was having a transfusion peeked into her room to see the lady who actually had a hemoglobin of four. Mania plagued her exhausted brain until she was too weak from breast cancer to care.

Yet the conflict ended. She healed. I hear the echo of her life like background music. Some of the words she mumbled in her last hours render all of the thrashing conflict obsolete.

"Wow! Amazing! Great! You did that? Is this a holiday? You're nice to hold my hand. What are we celebrating? I've never seen that before. I have everything."

Shine

Life is hard.

Were you hoping it would be easy?

Today I listened to a friend talk about the pain in her marriage. She is a warm, caring woman with enough love to light up a whole room with her laugh. Her capacity for compassion makes her easy to trust and to confide in. I do it regularly.

Yet even someone whose heart is wide open cannot always connect to her own husband. Why is it like this?

Perhaps you have had the experience of wrapping Christmas lights on a tree. If even one of them comes disconnected the whole string stays dark. Then you are forced to rummage along the wires until you find the broken bulb and replace it. This can take hours when you would rather be doing something much more interesting like sampling the cookies that just came out of the oven, or reading the colorful pile of cards accumulating in the kitchen from friends you have not heard from in awhile. But you want the tree to have lights, so you keep searching. Finally you find the culprit and replace it. Bling! The light sings out from your hands. I am not sure, but I think the other bulbs, the ones who were waiting for their chance to shine, are grateful too.

Sometimes there are parts of us, or the people we love, that are broken. For reasons they may not know they cannot make a loving connection through words or touch. This does not always mean they do not love us, it can simply mean that a part of them is damaged.

"Arise, shine; for your light is come, and the glory of the LORD is risen upon you. For, behold, the darkness shall cover the earth, and gross darkness the people: but the LORD shall arise upon you, and his glory shall be seen upon you. And the Gentiles shall come to your light, and kings to the brightness of your rising."

Isaiah 60

Incompatible

John and I have a slew of differences. I let the fruit bowl and spoon jar flank the stove, because I love to sense their beauty when I cook. He moves them to the butcher block because he thinks the heat will damage the fruit or ignite the spoons. The vessels travel forth and back, depending on who currently rules the kitchen.

John likes the lights to be dim in our bedroom and on the computer screen. He tugs the curtains and clicks the smaller sun icon. I am thirsty for sunshine in the morning and a sharp image when I write so I pull it back and tattoo the larger sun icon.

Our cupboards are another point of dissension. He prefers them to be full to capacity and lugs home eight grocery bags when he shops. Last month there were twelve jars of peanut butter before he stopped grabbing a couple more just in case. I prefer to use up the last can of pintos, or see the back of the freezer, so I can be sure of eating food from the current presidency.

I read about a couple who argued about whether to put glasses pointing up or down on the shelf. Finally they decided to duke out their logic.

"I think they should go facing up so that the last bit of water won't drip on the shelf paper," he said.

"I think they should face down so that no dust gets in them," his wife retorted.

They were both convinced and traded practices.

Marriage is a yoke of two people who inevitably have skewed styles. Sleep schedules, spending habits, and a quota for social life can feel like a cleaver between you.

A friend told me about a debate he went to where the speakers began by articulating the other person's views. One was defending heterosexual marriage and the other was speaking for same sex relationships. My friend was struck by the willingness to cross the divide with understanding. Different beliefs did not negate respect.

Someday when the we are pressed through the sieve of death, our opinions will be too congealed to slip through the pinprick holes. Only the compassion will be fluid enough to wash into eternity.

"If people would make love to the Lord and charity toward the neighbor the principal of faith, doctrinal matters would then be only varieties of opinion. Truly Christian people would leave everyone to follow his or her conscience, and would say in their hearts that a person is truly a Christian when she or he lives as the Lord teaches. Thus from all the differing churches there would be made one church; and all the dissensions that come forth from doctrine alone would vanish; yea, all hatreds of one against another would be dissipated in a moment, and the Lord's kingdom would come upon the earth."

Emanuel Swedenborg, *Heavenly Secrets* 1799

Dragon

I made a quilt for Zachary that has twelve dragons on it. They are different colors, with a variety of foes defending turreted castles. He is my third son to be enthralled with battle. I read Hardy Boys books to Lukas by the hour, the entire Redwall series to Micah, and the Eragon trilogy to Zack. They apparently arrived in my arms with an insatiable thirst for heroes. My daughters too begged for books about Laura and Mary defending their cabin from a blizzard, or Anne of Green Gables conquering the hearts of terse Marilla and silent Matthew.

Why is this?

I suppose if I had foreknowledge that my child was going to be bushwacked by a dragon, or orphaned, I would invest in strategies to prepare them. One tactic would be to drench their imaginations with stories of bravery, rich with sword wielding mice and plucky school mistresses. It would be prudent to nudge them to practice for hours and years, like bow tethered boys with homemade arrows that would not pierce cold butter.

It seems inevitable that marriages are besieged by insidious dragons too. The shapes vary enough to disarm the most watchful couples. Misunderstandings jab between the cracks of our plated armor, and fiery accusations singe our fleshy limbs.

I am thirsty for images of couples who have outsmarted the dragons of self importance, or loosened the tongues of mute spouses. The other day was a quiet one for John and I, gaping with long stretches sans words. I had let slip a barbed comment that slammed shut the portals of communication.

Perhaps that is why the Parent of all children embedded in our hearts the craving to defend long before the first flashing blade sliced the smoky air. If we wait to google fencing when the dragon's fiery breath is licking under the door it may be too late.

Defensive

As I have mentioned before Benjamin is learning to wash his own hair. This morning his teacher called mid day. I always bristle when her name comes up on caller ID. My mind raced to both fictional and non fictional scenarios.

"He threw up. Come get him ASAP."

"He forgot his back pack again."

"Why didn't you send in money for the field trip?"

My imagination usually spices up the words exchanged with a few recriminations lurking between the marginally polite ones.

"You are a sorry excuse for a mother. Why did you send him in sick? What do you think we are, an infirmary?"

"It does not take a rocket scientist to remember a back pack. Focus, woman."

"I already know that you are forgetful and cheap, but get a grip lady. Fork over the twenty bucks."

Today she said that they had noticed small white specks in his hair. They wondered if it was lice.

My memory rocketed back to torturous, month long ordeals involving relentless combing, meticulous washing and nasty potions. I steeled myself for the verdict.

"But it wasn't. We realized it was clumps of shampoo. Clearly he is struggling with rinsing well. We wondered if we could take him to the hair cutters and get him a buzz."

A flood of feelings flashed through my body, involving shame, defensiveness and protectiveness for his mop of sandy hair.

I could practically hear the teachers snickering about my inept parenting, probably using my photo as a dart board.

"Could John and I talk about it? We will help him get his hair clean tonight."

Defensiveness makes sense if you are a baby gosling in a lion preserve. But it can get in the way of an otherwise functional relationship. The teachers at Ben's school want to help him succeed, and that can involve pointing things out that I don't want to hear.

The other day I felt a need to say something to John that I could predict he did not want to hear. Boiled down to five words, I thought I could ease it into the conversation without sinking his self esteem ship. But he went down like the Titanic. The rest of the day was awkward. He stayed up late on the computer, a symptom of feeling wounded.

I felt annoyed at how difficult it was to give him simple information. Then I remembered the residual shampoo. All his teacher was doing was giving me information, so I could help Benjamin succeed in the future.

I would think harder about this but Benjamin is late to school and if I don't find his back pack I will be in the doghouse again.

Litmus Test

I was talking with a friend who is committed to her marriage. I think I can even say she is more committed now than she was when she said "I do". That is in part because her love for her husband has grown, but also because of the stress she feels from watching marriages around her shrivel up. Her husband has thirteen divorces on his family tree. She has watched the thinly masked pain of all those children who are not sure who to invite and who to leave out at a family gathering.

She told me that she has a litmus test for making decisions.

"Does it support us staying together?"

When faced with the conveyor belt of choices endemic in life on planet earth, she asks this clarifying question. It has a way of sifting out the extraneous details, vying for our attention.

Do we move or stay where we are?

Do I send my kids to this school or that one?

Do we go out or stay home with the kids?

The question is like the switchman at the train tracks in the last century, who had the power to send engines either to the left or to the right. At the flip of his switch he could alter the direction of a steaming locomotive barreling through at a hundred miles an hour carrying as many passengers only dimly aware of their own bearings.

Her priority is not about the money, or the prestige, impressing the neighbors or fitting in. It is about her marriage.

She and her husband went away for the weekend this fall. She orchestrated child care far in advance, and chose a place to go. Still she felt like the destination did not matter much.

"We could stay in a cardboard box in Philly, just so we were together."

I admire her clarity. The world tugs on us in a thousand ways, imploring us for time, resources and loyalty. Yet this clarion call keeps her headed toward the goal she holds most dear.

First Impression

I remember learning about the study of baby ducks in psychology class. A man made sure he was the first thing the ducklings saw when they cracked open their eggshells and *Voila*, he was "Mom" to them for life.

I think it was about imprinting, which is next of kin to impressions. We humans latch on to first impressions and hang on for dear life too. I know I have.

Once a repairman treated me particularly well and I have been hiking back to his store, past several others, for years. This last job did seem a bit sub par, in that he fixed the broken plug with tape instead of replacing it, which I might have expected considering the bill of $125, but I notice my first impression of him looms large in spite of it. To not bring my small problems to him would feel like a little duck turning away from Mom and snuffing.

"I can find a better Mother than you."

I am vaguely aware of impressions I have made on people.

My house has never been what you would call pristine. It is a good bet that if you are sitting on the couch and suddenly need a pen for doing homework there are several writing implements between the cushions to choose from. I have often browsed the house after emptying the dishwasher and found enough dirty specimens lying around to fill it completely. We have not been in the running with say my daughter's friend's mother. Mercy came home one day with fresh eyes as to the possibilities for living standards.

"Mom, even her spices are in alphabetical order."

So one day an elderly lady decided she would march over to my house to teach me and my kids a thing or two about chores. At that slender slice in time, I did have in place one of oodles of attempts for corralling kids to work. I wrote a list of jobs and left it on the table. Each kid had to do two before they could play. The upshot was, kids sprang out of bed to get the lamest tasks available.

The woman and I were having tea, in perfectly clean cups I might add, when the first two kids woke up. They tore past us to snatch the list and began taking out trash cans. Two more kids appeared bleary eyed and moaned.

"Awww, I wanted to take out the trash." The woman's eyes got big. She had not expected such eager beavers at the Odhner house. She did not realize that after the approximately four minute bout of industrious behavior, the kids settled in for twelve hours of uninterrupted play. Not only that the entire system withered after a few weeks.

Sometimes we have misplaced impressions of other couples. They look as if their life is charmed, with ne'er an ill word between them. We came to the conclusion after solid research, say the three minutes we spent with them at a party, or the information gleaned from twelve consecutive years of Christmas cards.

But we may be prudent to remember that not all first impressions are spot on. And I like to go back to what I read on a bumper sticker.

"What other people think of you is none of your business."

Keep Score

There is a game of equilibrium that shows up for me at Christmas. I want to predict the size and cost of every gift that comes in my direction, and send one of comparable value first. This is difficult to juggle when dealing with office mates, friends, relatives and family. Sometimes the discrepancy is small, and can be overlooked. But other times I am given a present from someone when I was not expecting it, and I wish I had a spare fruitcake in my pocket.

This year there were some quaintly well matched gifts amidst the web of offerings in which I took part. I gave my son a mug made by Zazzle. He gave me one too. My coworker made me a felt ornament. I handed one to her. There was no need for supplemental gifting, like there was the year my brother in law gave the twins exquisitely embroidered wool capes, and I gave him a rock.

I admit it was a rock, but not merely one I scraped up from the mud. I bought it in a store, and it doubled as a candle holder but still despite its hefty weight it did not score well on the what-I-give-you-equals-what-you-gave-us scale.

Marriage is an ongoing flow of exchanges. This includes acts of kindness, rescues, paychecks and wrapped gifts. The variety makes score keeping more complicated than trying to follow twelve concurrent volleyball tournaments. For instance, the toilet upstairs clogged on Christmas eve. All things plumbing fall into John's domain, for some unspoken reason that I have no interest in challenging. Somehow fixing that problem counted like a thoughtfully chosen pair of earrings under the tree, which there wasn't one of. In fact there was nothing under the tree from John. To anyone. He explained that the new roof over our heads was gift enough, and if you are talking pure numbers I must admit that he did out price the whole pile.

Watching the score is indeed tempting. It readies my mind for the expectation of what I deserve. But when two people finally learn how to give everything with a generous heart, there is no score board yet invented that can keep track of their winnings.

Can We Come In Too?

There is a sweet yet confusing story in the New Testament about young women who want to go to a wedding. Five of them were allowed to come in and five were not. I remember thinking as a child that it was mean to shut out those girls. I would certainly have opened the door for them. Even if it was past my bedtime.

The ones who were invited in had oil in their lamps while the others had empty vessels. They were told to go and fill their lamps and then they could come too.

John explained the story to me as one not of random exclusion but of preparation. Getting ready for marriage is as important as preparation for a job, or parenthood. It is reasonable for a potential employer to admit people who have adequately studied for a position while refusing those who are ill suited. Although babies are born to women who have readied themselves through reading, good nutrition and prenatal care as well as women who have not, things usually go much better in the first scenario.

There are colleges and high schools that now offer relationship education. Although the programs are new, many are quite popular. It makes sense to learn things that can help people navigate such an important decision as who to marry.

The lamps in the story needed oil to keep burning. Marriage needs love in order to live. Oil gives light, and warmth and provides a lubricant for reducing friction. When we are kind to our partner the friction goes down as well.

"At that time the kingdom of heaven will be like ten virgins who took their lamps and went out to meet the bridegroom. Five of the virgins were foolish, and five were wise. When the foolish ones took their lamps, they did not take extra oil with them. But the wise ones took flasks of olive oil with their lamps. The bridegroom was delayed a long time and they all became drowsy and fell asleep. But at midnight there was a shout, 'Look, the bridegroom is here! Come out to meet him.' Then all the virgins woke up and trimmed their lamps. The foolish ones said to the wise, 'Give us some of your oil, because our lamps are going out.' 'No,' they replied. 'There won't be enough for you and for us. Go instead to those who sell oil and buy some for yourselves.' But while they had gone to buy it, the bridegroom arrived, and those who were ready went inside with him to the wedding banquet. Then the door was shut. Later, the other virgins came too, saying, 'Lord, lord! Let us in' But he replied, 'I tell you the truth, I do not know you!' Therefore stay alert, because you do not know the day or the hour."

Matthew 25

What Was Your Yesterday?

The other day I was speaking with a friend who had figured something out. Her parents, still living, had given a big chunk of their attention to their marriage as she was growing up. She noticed that she had chosen to give a larger portion of time to her young children. Her husband's father on the other hand had died when he was young, so he grew up watching his mother be alone. He was often urging his wife to pay more attention to him than she already was.

This has been a source of conflict for years. She felt like they could wait until the kids were a little older, and he had an unspoken fear that waiting could be a mistake. Neither of them were wrong. Both of them were responding from their own experience.

Giving attention to your young children is a splendid thing. Making time for your marriage is also a wise plan. It can be a juggle to pull both of them off. What touched me most was this woman's ability to climb out of her own world view long enough to see life from her husband's eyes. That takes empathy. Sometimes we are reluctant to do so, because it may invalidate our own stance. But two sides of an issue can actually be a fuller picture. If you have ever tried to drive with one eye shut you know what a handicap it is. Depth perception is gone. Peripheral vision suffers drastically.

Her perception did not make the issue disappear. But it did unlock some of the underlying currents. That can be helpful. She may or may not give voice to her husband about what she realized. But the compassion will soften her actions in a way that may foster compromise.

We sometimes think we married one person, and that his or her past has no influence. But we are more prudent to look at those pasts, and unpack the ways they continue to influence us now.

Because family patterns determine how you start out, but they do not have to predict where you end up.

Near Miss

We bought new IPhones a couple of years ago and the old one was sitting around. When my son in California heard that, he asked if we would mail it to his father-in-law to use, after which he would sell it on ebay for us. It sounded like a plan. Lukas texted me the address and I headed to the post office fifteen minutes before it closed for the weekend. As I was packing it up another person arrived in line behind me. I dislike keeping people waiting and got flustered about how long I was taking. Quickly I put the phone in the little box and the little box in the medium box, with the label and postage, thanked the post lady and gathered up my things from the counter.

I headed out for a couple of other errands, and when I got to the bank I checked my phone for messages.

"AAAAAAKKKK!" I had mailed the wrong phone!! I zoomed back to the post office, thinking I should call John to beat me to the post office before it closed but oops... my phone was at the bottom of a pile of packages headed for Colorado. I drove as fast as I dared and screeched into the parking lot. There was one car left. I banged on the door and called.

"Maria!!! I know you are closed, but I mailed the wrong

phone!!!" She unlocked the door and poked her head out.

"I am so sorry but could I change the phone in that package I just sent? Please?" She was clearly annoyed but she let me into the secret room where packages are kept before the truck swallows them up, and she dug through the pile until she found it. I thanked her and opened the box, snatched out my dear phone and replaced it with the old one. I even kissed it.

"Thank you so much!!" I let out a sigh of relief and went back to doing errands.

Now I remember that I had a meaningful life for upwards of forty five years without owning a cell phone. It can be done. But I have become accustomed to the convenience of instant communication, hand held internet connection and a myriad of other tricks, though far fewer apps than my sons employ on their phones. Going back to pre phone days would feel like a sacrifice. Maybe I believe I deserve a phone.

But do I? Deserving creeps into marriage, and can erode our sense of gratitude. I am more grateful for my phone today than I was last week. Losing it brought that sentiment up from the bottom of the pile. Coming close to losing your marriage can also be the occasion for a spike in gratitude.

I just read an article about how couples in distress can separate for a few months, as a means of reconciliation. In the case of one therapist, it brought healing to half of the marriages who tried it.

But you can use a simpler version. Just announce that you are escaping to Colorado, and then hide yourself in a big box with a ribbon.

Always Watching

I think God is pretty slick to have invented children. Grown ups who may or may not feel inclined to clean up their act, or drive safely are suddenly yanked into self submission simply because their kids are watching.

Recently a woman told me she was thick into berating her husband when she noticed that his personal fan club, namely their kids, was aghast. She saw herself in the mirror and did not like what she saw. Screaming at her husband was one thing but demeaning her children's father in their presence was another.

I heard a man tell about a conversation when his wife drove the kids to school one day, an errand he usually took on. His little girl asked their mother "Where are all the idyuts today?" Apparently their father had things to say about his fellow commuters often enough that the kids wondered what had happened to them when their mom drove.

Many of us have had occasion to see a three year old perch her hands on her hips, furrow her brow and speak sharply to the dog in exactly the same tone her mother uses when conferring discipline. Embarrassing to say the least. I had my own comeuppance when my little boy scolded me.

"Mommy Joshua Odhner!!" Apparently I use his middle name, which I chose with abundant adoration, as an indicator of retribution.

It is helpful, if not exactly comfortable, to have feedback. I wonder what would shift in the world if there were no mirrors. Would we all abandon any concern for personal appearance? Would that be a good thing? Certainly entire hair, cosmetic and fashion industries would crumble.

What would happen if we stayed oblivious to our own behaviors? We could continue to bumble along, insulting and contradicting with abandon. Who could expect more from a socially blind person? But instead we have children watching us, and friends who are brave enough to reflect what they see.

It's ouchy, but better than remaining in the dark.

The Apple Man

This is the Apple Man. He sells honeycrisps so sweet that people have been known to drive many miles and stand in long lines to get them, even before they plunk their money down. I know someone who went two hours each way to buy twelve cases.

The Apple Man did not come to market today, because honeycrisps aren't on the trees in January. His branches are empty.

But he isn't worried, having seen winters aplenty. Waiting does not frighten him. He will take care of the orchards in the meantime, pruning and fertilizing.

He looks happy to be selling them to eager customers, after months of labor and watching tiny promises grow into fruit. He has more than he can eat personally, so he brings them to the Farmer's Market and trades them for cash. I would venture to say that he is proud of his crop and feels good about the time he spent coaxing apples to grow.

He looks like he has been at it a few years, and has learned some tricks about worms and bees. I could ask him some of those practices, and he would likely be cheerful about passing them on. But I would be better off following him in his orchards, month after month. Wisdom is not easily transferred in a five minute conversation, and experience never is.

Someone could be fooled into thinking that his job is easy: just pick apples and rake in the dough. But his story is longer than that, beginning with seeds and grafting, tilling and irrigation. He spent many lonely hours, long before anyone even predicted they would want apples next fall. He dealt with problems I will never give a second thought to as I sink my teeth into the juicy flesh.

Marriage is a place for fruit and growing too. Sometimes we notice another smiling couple, perhaps at a party, and think they have an easy time of it. We are blind to the months and years of effort that preceded this moment of sweetness. Perhaps there were stretches of loneliness, working with a relationship that felt empty, and habits that had to be pruned away. Probably wormy feelings came wiggling in, and they had to learn how to deter them. There was cross fertilization of honeyed ideas from other blooming marriages. Maybe the waiting for warmth frightened them, when it went on longer than they were expecting.

Yet here they are now, laughing and touching. I could ask them about it, and they would look at each other and wonder what to say, what to leave out.

But wisdom is not easily transferred in a five minute conversation, and experience never is.

"There is a knowledge of the way through walking in it, and a walking in the way through knowledge of it."
Emanuel Swedenborg, *Divine Providence* 60

Two of Me

Dear Lord,

Sometimes it feels as if there are two of me. Two feelings, pulling in different directions. Do I speak my mind, even if it may hurt my spouse? Do I keep quiet and work on changing myself? Do I need to say everything I feel, or can some things that began as urgent messages, simply expire? Can you gradually, not too quickly, please, meld the two of me into the one of me?

Guardian Angels

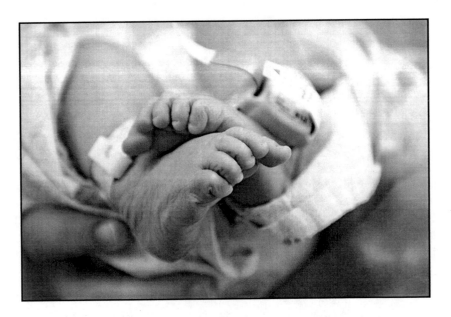

I believe in angels. I suppose many people do, yet I have a suspicion that folks divide when it comes to job descriptions.

Some subscribe to the Security Guard model. The cherub on duty peruses a dozen monitors at once. He or she is loosely aware of the comings and goings of the earthlings in his or her care, and if any trouble flares up sends in a deputy.

Others lean toward the Roman Gladiator format. Heavenly hosts watch us from the stands, cheering when we conquer the lions in our lives, and heaving a collective groan when we are devoured.

Then there is the Disneyland prototype. These attendants are cordial enough, willing to give us directions, pick up our trash and explain the rules, but they do not go so far as to know our names. And if you come back two hours later there is a different shift working.

I heard about a cave in New Mexico that is a popular hang out for bats. On a given day there will be seven hundred thousand creatures there. At night the moms go out to do their bat shopping, leaving a few babysitters behind, and when they return to the vast, inky black cave amidst the swarm of four inch brown balls of fur, each mother manages to find her own baby bat.

I am unwilling to stomach that God gives such particular attention to the care of bats and leaves us humans to the whim of whomever is on duty.

I also trust that angels love marriage. They are even more motivated to help us find eternal love than we are, sort of like how I get way more excited about my kids being kind than they are. Just the other day, I was feeling overwhelmed about the children's program I was trying to put on for fifty kids. All the details, and last minute changes were swirling around in my leaky brain.

"I am scared that it won't work."

"Let's pray, Mom." Hope and Aurelle closed their sweet brown eyes and curled their arms around me.

"Oh Lord, please help Mom to do a good job on this children's program. Help all the kids to have a great time and not get sad or lost. Amen." Wooosh. The anxiety seeped out of me and into the absorbent ground.

These are the same girls who pray every night to have good marriages, and be good wives. They just think they are saying an ordinary prayer, but I am moved by their innocence every single night.

And I wouldn't mind having angels like them on my watch.

Talking About the Weather

Current troubles are plentiful. The weather alone is consuming a bunch of attention, both from people trying to escape it as well as those trying to maneuver its effects. I fall into the former category, not being inclined to heroism on a grand scale. I know people who are. They go out into the rain and snow on purpose to look for and retrieve complete strangers. I bet there is an extra cushy place in heaven for them. But then again maybe they have enough mettle to last into the next few centuries and would be disappointed by complete refuge. I suppose God could create a little bit of danger to keep them sharp.

I asked John if he was scared of all the uncertainty. He smiled and said he is a good friend of the Person in charge of wind and waves. I calmed down a notch, but I am still wishing the trees beside our house were shorter. Or made of rubber.

I notice that the kids are only afraid if we lend them ours. The rain has not actually started as I write this. They look puzzled by me bringing lawn chairs into the house, and obsessing on news videos.

The thing I try to hold front and center is the memory of past disasters that actually melted into a new way of life. My mother lost everything in a flood, and she moved in with me. My baby was hospitalized for severe failure to thrive and had a hundred appointments before his first birthday. But if I ask at the Christmas table who wants Benjamin to be part of our family every hand bolts to the sky. He currently is into texting. His siblings vie for his messages, and answer them on the sly even if they are in a meeting with the boss. I was flattened by three kids in diapers, especially as I was using cloth ones. The bathroom smelled pretty bad. I cannot actually think of a silver lining for that one except that it is over.

Hard times are at the heart of any story. I suppose it is part of creating a character more resilient than a butterfly.

One of the miracles of marriage and family is that we get to turn toward each other instead of away.

Change

One of the ways we limit each other is to believe we cannot change. We can keep ourselves stuck, as well as the people we love.

"My husband never goes to parties."

"I can't figure out computers."

It can be helpful to frame those observations as current rather than predictive.

"Up until now my husband has chosen not to go to many social events."

"I have not learned how to use a computer yet."

The other day I heard of a person who is training for a marathon. He said this about himself.

Couch to 11 miles (8 minute mile/barefoot) in a little over 16 months... if I did it, anyone can do it!

That affects how I hear his achievement, seeing as I am still on the couch. The same day I heard of a couple who were in distress, whose response to the suggestion of offering each other a few minutes of appreciations was sarcasm.

"Us? Appreciate each other? Not a chance."

Then a scant month later they were going on an overnight get away together.

I notice that parents usually refrain from boxing in their growing children.

"Martha is eleven months old and cannot walk. I don't think she ever will learn."

"Charlie grabs all the toys when he goes to a friend's house. He will always be a selfish brat."

We can do ourselves a disservice as well, when we deny the possibility of change.

"I have fallen out of love with my husband. It is over."

"I cannot figure out how he thinks. I never will."

Considering the effort God goes to to surround us with constant growth in nature this is a surprising response. The only skies that never change are the ones in a photograph.

One Letter At a Time

One letter at a time. It can seem tedious. A skilled typist can snap out five hundred characters a minute without breaking a sweat. Yet the effort feels too puny to take on a whole manuscript, or a biography. There are, all told, only twenty six letters to work with. Capitals and punctuation stretch the possibilities for meaning. But the letters themselves fit on a child's set of blocks, or in an alphabet book with aardvarks and zebras.

Back when people used typewriters, I had one whose e no longer had the oomph to print the paper. So when I looked over the paragraphs, there were spaces sprinkled amid most of the words where the e did not show up. It was hard to decipher. What was I trying to say?

My life sometimes feels chopped into individual key strokes... this spoon washed, that sandwich made. Do they string together to create something of more significance than their ephemeral worth?

Where are the letters with which I compose a marriage? I buy carrots, because John likes them. Done. I wash his socks because he has run out. Snap. I find his barbershop tie, or try to, because he is late for a show. Bang. I smile at him across the room, because it warms him. Click. I hold his hand in the dark. Press.

Do those small motions say anything? Do they construct meaning within the ribbons of time?

It feels monotonous, with its clicking repetition. But what else would I use? These small kindnesses are some of the few dozen actions that blend together to spell a lifetime... soft words, a touch, warm soup, sitting side by side. How many ways are there? If I were to omit the carrots, or the socks, it would leave holes in my story.

But together, the very runes weave the tale of *The Love of Husband and Wife*.

Hidden By the Night

Everything disappears when night falls. Our eyes cannot discern the individual needles on an evergreen, or a sparrow in the branches. And when we cannot see something, it is gone. Right?

Before my parents realized I was near sighted as a teenager, the world was fuzzy. I remember believing that if I could not see those people across the room very well, they could not see me either. Then mom took me for an eye test, and the world suddenly came into focus with glasses.

"How about that! I can read the small print on the chalk board now." I thought with surprise. I felt as if the letters suddenly came into being, when they were there all along.

There is a renowned test by Piaget where he shows a child a ball, and then hides it under a pillow. The little boy or girl believes that the ball no longer exists. Psychologists find this way of thinking fascinating, in its imperfection.

"Try looking under the pillow," urges the tester. With unbridled glee, the child discovers that the ball is real again. Whether it was gone and came back, or never really left does not matter. The ball is here now, and it is time to play.

Love comes barreling into our hearts when we are first married. We see our partner as lovely and loveable. The world is bright, and we are certain it will stay that way.

Then, when we forget to notice the faithful message of the earth's rotation, darkness falls. Love grows dim.

"Something is terribly wrong. My love is gone, because I cannot see it anymore."

An adolescent relationship, one that has not fully matured yet, can be duped by the illusion that something you cannot see has vanished for good. Our partner looks less appealing in shadow. We are still who we always were, but he or she has diminished somehow.

Another thing that retreats with the light is warmth. A few years into marriage the feelings grow cooler. Somehow we manage to miss the constant reminder of changing seasons, and the earth's shifting temperature.

"Spring will come in April, but my affection for my partner is lost forever," the inky thoughts slink in.

Angels find these thoughts sad, in their imperfection.

"Try looking harder for it," they urge. Then we slip on the new glasses, the ones that help to correct our skewed vision.

Suddenly we rediscover our love. Whether it was gone and came back, or was simply hiding does not matter. It is here now, and it is time to play.

Continental Drift

When January begins, you've been given a new year. It stretches out in front of you like a virgin snowfall, waiting to be explored. Soon there will be trails of footsteps, some bold with far apart prints, others halting, retraced or abruptly changing direction. Some will show groups of footprints all tangled together in varying sizes. The silent stories chronicle times traveled with others, with all the blessings and bothers that entails. They also mark the solitary steps, perhaps with the dimple left by a walking stick, visually changing the rhythm from a two step to a waltz.

A year can feel like a vast expanse in which to cover ground. Or, looking back over your shoulder, last year's steps can look rather paltry, hardly visible in the shadows and valleys, disappearing beneath the forces of wind, water and time.

Time is an elusive barometer of accomplishment. Kipling beckons us to "Fill the unforgiving minute with sixty seconds worth of distance run." Certainly twelve months would afford us an impressive distance indeed, were we in the business of moving off road vehicles or a pair of Nikes. But what if we are more interested in transporting a house, or a relationship? How much time does it take to forgive an old grudge, or to launch a dream?

One of my gifts this Christmas was to forego criticism of my husband for a year. Will there be any visible footsteps to show the progress I have made when I turn around next December and survey where I have come? Perhaps it will feel like I have traveled at the speed of continental drift. No doubt it will have been an expensive present, costing me dearly as the plates of my rocky soul build up pressure beneath the surface.

But sometimes, after centuries of silence, those land masses shift to create whole new formations, losing old ones beneath the foam. Dare I hope that after 365 days of swallowed comments, there might erupt in me a mountain on whose pinnacle I might stand? Could it be that having never moved a foot I may have gained a thousand?

Round We Go

The view from the top of a Ferris wheel is different from the one at the bottom.

At the apex, you can peer across the carnival, taking in the whole scene. In that upward swing where you are almost weightless you are poised for a scant moment, brushing the floor of heaven. In less time than it takes to talk about it, you can feel as if you are launched into the expanse.

Then you propel downwards again, where the mass of people and popcorn is so thick it seems impossible that there is room for this rickety cart carrying you. You are immersed in a thicket of people, and noise and trinkets. The crowd presses against your eyes and ears, with a thousand glitzy details all grabbing for your attention: the cones of hot pink cotton candy, the ticket seller yelling to customers, the baby crying in a stroller, the blinking lights.

Abruptly the chains clank under the strain and pull you back up to the clouds, where every detail fades, all crowds are shushed, and you are transported again into the big wide sky. You can see across the throngs, and their power to overwhelm you falls away. There is only you, and the person you are riding with to absorb the beauty.

But the chains pull you down again, and the mire swallows

you.

Round and round you ride, between two worlds.

Marriage feels like that. Sometimes John and I will have a peak experience entertaining friends. The meal was delightful, the conversations were lofty, the partnership between us was at its height. We serve and smile, buoyed up by our shared desire to make these people happy. Then the guests wave goodbye and as the door shuts we are thrust into the piles of dishes, and garbage, and uneaten food. Suddenly we scrabble with the details and annoyance of cleaning up the remains. Our company has barely started their car before we are entrenched again in the hot pink feelings and the cries of neglected children.

Once our small girl even asked, "Are the customers gone?"

Other times we work hard to create an event, such as church or a marriage group. Last Easter we worked for weeks making a hundred fluttering butterflies on straws and strings, and a dozen costumes for children. We hammered at the details of buying live butterflies online, and dealt with the litter of paper across the table as we cut out Painted Ladies. Then as the service began, we were lifted above the particulars, and into the magic of all those pieces taking off. The room was carried up with the wonder of dancing children, noiseless butterflies, and the miracle that is Easter.

Up and down, around and back again we whirl with yanking speed. Is the feeling of euphoria real if it disappears so quickly? Perhaps I would be wiser to ask if the mundane emotions are substantial. Their reign is short lived too, and more likely to evaporate over time. Even now I can conjure up the thrill of those butterflies, and the lively dinners.

But the paper scraps and leftovers are somewhere down under my feet.

Under Dog

It is hard being the under dog.

But hey, it is no picnic being the over dog either.

This year I hid Easter baskets for my kids. As always, I try to predict that vacillating line between oppressively difficult and pathetically easy. Then I have to sit on my hands while they are looking and getting discouraged. My heart rate accelerated when our daughter walked right by the cupboard her basket was lurking behind.

"Do I rush in and show her where it is?"

"Can I give a subtle hint?"

Their memories are set on short term, or they would remember from the last umpty years that they will eventually find it and yes it will be worth the effort once they swoop into the jellybeans and chocolate.

But for what feels like forever they wander, checking the same corners I hid them in last time, hoping it will be simple. Benjamin looked at me with droopy eyes, as if this were unfair punishment instead of a game.

Then Hope's eye catches the corner of pink, and she screams with excitement.

The success in the kitchen ratchets up the determination of her twin in the living room. Aurelle finally spots hers under the pile of sweaters and shoes, and all discouragement evaporates as she takes out each treasure and savors the bounty.

I wonder how God feels as He sets us on the hunt for a good marriage. Just yesterday John asked me to do something for him. It was not ridiculously easy, but neither was it Herculean. I thought of my kids' wilting enthusiasm while searching for baskets, and determined I would be less wimpy.

John and I finished the task, and I enjoyed the sweetness of having helped him. It was even better than chocolate.

Content Yet?

Why does it look like everyone else but me is having a great ol' time?

"They have the job, the house, the marriage, the dream. What do I have? I hear their laughter, but I am not included. I have a boring life. Everyone else has a perfect life."

If we could actually see the shadows of the miscreants who whisper such absurdities in our ears, we would be appalled. I suspect that they are misshapen, ghoulish and sound like chalk skidding on a chalkboard. Nothing about them would suggest integrity, and we would dismiss them as easily as I do phone solicitors.

"Mrs. Odhner, this is your golden opportunity to invest in lakefront property in southern Florida... "

Yeah right. My neighbors would be eight foot alligators, and the humidity would poach an egg.

So why are many of us duped by the absurdities that slither into our minds when we were otherwise minding our own business?

One of the interesting perks about having a son with autism is noticing that he is immune to such lies. Jealousy finds no purchase in his thinking. On Christmas morning he is quite content with the contents of his stocking, and it would not occur to him to expect anything. Even amidst the confusion of eight siblings passing bright gifts to each other, he expresses no need for more. On the contrary, his older brothers and sisters, who have taken great pains and big bucks to find the perfect Toy Story truck or Lego kit to ignite his million dollar smile, have to coax his attention away from the pack of cards he has been playing with since eight o'clock.

What would it be like if all of us were satisfied with what lay in our lap?

There is a song by the group Acappella that I have listened to for perhaps twenty years. It seems to come on just when I am falling prey to those grumbling doubts.

"His divine power has given us everything, everything we need."

It is a calm place to be when I can get there, that oasis of acceptance. Not only that... it is true.

Trampoline

What is a trampoline for... exercise or fun?

There was a tramp at the end of my one block road growing up. It had no net, and no adult supervision that I can remember. But we kids would bounce for hours, using games like Three X's or China Wall to increase our memory and endurance. We thought it was all about playing, but in the meantime we spent time outdoors, learned to share and follow rules, and increased our cardiovascular health. We got a workout, every time.

Is marriage about getting stronger, or fun? Last night I would have said the latter. John and I were smiling and bantering back and forth about an inside joke, enjoying the cozy fire and listening to music. But last week, when we were trying to book nine flights to California on four different dates out of three airports, using frequent flyer miles on two different airlines, with companion coupons and as few dollars as possible, our marriage was getting a workout. We struggled to be kind while being efficient, yet still following the rules and staying on task. It was exhausting.

I suppose if I were a hermit, and never had to share a meal or a car or a bathroom with anyone, I could still evolve spiritually. I guess. But if I am planning on increasing my heart's capacity to love, I may as well do it in a way that is fun too.

Generosity

Many people have heard the fairy tale of the king who gets mad at the queen, who gets mad at the maid, who gets mad at the princess, who gets mad at the dog. There are embellishments but that is the gist of it.

Negative feelings can spread as fast as chicken pox, but so can good ones.

This summer my twins made friends with a little girl from Canada. They played non stop for the three days they were together, mostly involving dolls. They have the one they got from the thrift store, and the girl across the street has three so the four girls made out just fine. But the girl from Canada kept saying she wished she owned one too. After she was gone the three girls made a pact to earn a hundred dollars to buy her one.

They fed a neighbor's fish and made the first chunk. Then they landed a cat feeding job and they were closer to their goal. One of them got the idea to have a lemonade stand and they started squeezing every lemon to be found on our little cul-de-sac. They made a cardboard sign and handed out fresh, if a bit thin lemonade for two dimes. We moms replenished supplies and they added cookies to the menu. In all there were four days of selling refreshments to the locals. One afternoon, Hope said how fun it was to get to know the neighbors, and their licky dogs. I agreed.

Several people mentioned that they had bought lemonade and gotten a spontaneous hug to boot. None of the patrons knew the recipient of the doll but it still spread sweetness to see generosity in action. Several handed them a dollar and did not ask for change. One woman heard about it and missed the lemonade but saw them jumping on the trampoline and added her own contribution to the cause.

My own family was touched as well. Their brother said he had not spent that much money on his own girlfriend. I noticed generosity seeping into my own behavior over the next few days. I said yes to seconds on ice cream.

I try to stretch my capacity for generosity. i have gifted a few people with quilts over the years, and sometimes I get cold feet at the end.

"Do I really want to give this away? It is so beautiful!!!" I hesitate. But it feels good to give, and I am crystal clear about the abundance I have been blessed with.

Being generous in your marriage can be hard, especially when you are feeling short changed. But opening the gates of lavishness can wash away the score keeping.

"Freely you have received, freely give."
Matthew 10

Recess

I heard on the news about the lack of recess in the daily schedule of Chicago schools.

Teachers argued that kids needed a chance to run around and play. They cited studies reporting the positive results of activity in an otherwise stationary routine. Parents rallied to demand a change. Yet the mayor cited the lack of funds to pay for the longer school day. What would they take out to make room for time on the playground? Math? Reading? Science?

Sure.

I am a fan of playing. In our marriage group last week we gave over the final ten minutes to an improv game. It was a great counterpoint to the discussion we had been having about male and female differences. The laughter was rich and genuine.

Sometimes couples forget the importance of recess in marriage. They feel swamped by the three C's of Children, Careers and Chores. But the research is definitive.

Having fun is serious business.

Prickly Outside, Sweet Inside

Eating a pineapple is a lot of work. Sometimes I have the pleasure of enjoying it after having wrestled with the spikes and tough skin. Usually though I take the wimp route and buy it in the can. Then I simply pretend that pineapple consumption carries no cost.

The interesting thing is, although I have not carried out any research, that the deliciousness factor actually increases with the effort expended.

Let me explain. Think about the Easter candy that took you half an hour to ferret out from between the tufts of grass it was nestled in. It was a ten, right? Whereas the lollipops that sit in a jar at the bank are a mere 2. I have watched children tromp vigorously through the back yard to find mediocre prizes in a treasure hunt, when those same trinkets would scarcely register as interesting if the kids stepped on them on the living room floor.

I think God knows this. Therefore it is in our best interest that the fruits of a marital relationship are shielded by spikes and tough skin. Otherwise it would be too easy.

I remember one time I was slogging through a prickly conversation to try to understand what John was saying. He was obviously upset about a tense board meeting. I was accelerating my efforts to find out what had transpired, and what the repercussions were. The louder I got, the less inclined he was to talk.

Finally, in a timid voice he said, "If I tell you why I am upset, then I will have to deal with your upset too."

I was stunned by the tenderness of his words. Here I was hacking away at his protective layer, when I realized that I was as threatening as the board members were.

That conversation, some fifteen years ago, still tastes sweet in my memory. I can picture where we were standing, and the wonder of finally understanding how he felt. Much as I cherish the fuzzy memories of gushing proclamations of adoration when we were falling in love, I do not remember them so clearly. There were a lot of romantic exchanges, but there was no struggle involved.

"I love you so much!"

"I love you even more, my darling!"

Yeah, it was cute and all. But it was too easy.

So bring on the prickly fruit. My sleeves are already rolled up.

La Luna

I invite you to go outside tonight to enjoy the moon. It will be the largest full moon to shine this year.

Moonlight has long been woven to romantic feelings. The Moonlight Sonata is a hauntingly beautiful piece.

Even if you and your sweetheart are not sitting side by side tonight, even if you do not yet know each other's names, you can take comfort in the fact that you wait under the same moon.

The moon stands guard as we sleep. It's light shimmies down through the clouds and branches, like a quiet serenade over a baby's cradle.

You do not need to speak, or be interesting as you lift your gaze skyward. It is enough just to feel small in the shadow of her majesty. She reigns tonight in her wordless watch, casting a glow over every roof, every spacious field, every bowed head. Whether you are aware or ignorant, thankful or apathetic, you are included in her glowing embrace.

The children's book *Many Moons* tells a tender story about how a father strives for the healing of his precious daughter by giving her the moon on a necklace. *The Prince of the Dolomites* is a story about a prince whose bride is from the moon. His beloved slowly withers with grief when she is forced to live away from its light, until he finds a way to harness it for her.

Both books tell how the power of love conquers seemingly impossible conundrums. Perhaps you can sit with your own troubles tonight, as you bask in the magic of her luminescence. Maybe there is a miracle waiting for you, too.

Dandelions

I deserve this husband!

Actually, I don't deserve him.

How is it possible that two completely contradictory statements can both rankle me?

I suppose it is because deserving has nothing to do with it.

We live in a complex society that depends largely on fair exchange. I give a specified amount of currency over the counter, they give me a pair of shoes. An employee shows up on the appointed days, stays until closing time and is mailed a paycheck. Occasionally some of us argue about the inequities of this system.

"You paid too much for that."

"I deserve a raise."

Much of the entire legal system is consumed with our attempts to even the balances of what people believe they deserve.

Yet there are forces among us that seem oblivious to this set of rules. The wildflowers that grace the roadsides appear without any observable human toil, and bestow their beauty on everyone who takes the time to look. The supply of loveliness seems inexhaustible.

One of the irresistible charms of babies rests in their capacity to adore their mothers regardless of beauty, personal grooming, wealth or any scale of performance on a given day.

Poor physical health, marital discord or tragedy may or may not seem linked logically to the choices we have made. Perhaps we fester with the notion that, if we somehow knew we deserved this, we could learn to live with our painful circumstances.

Yet the reverse is also unexpected. When we feel like we have merited the blessings that fall in our path, either by our efforts or sacrifice, the ceiling for joy is much lower than when it arrives unearned. The Lord seems partial to placing us in just this position of immunity to deserving.

"For He makes His sun rise on the evil and on the good, and sends rain on the just and on the unjust." Matt 5

When Jehovah gifted the children of Israel with manna every morning, the circumstances didn't follow our rules about equity.

"Some gathered much, some little. And when they measured it by the omer, those who gathered much did not have too much, and those who gathered little did not have too little. Each one gathered as much as he or she needed." Exodus 16

God gives to us not because we have somehow purchased His attention, but because we need it so desperately. It is not the fullness of our hands that inspires His mercy, it is because they are vacant.

"Ho, everyone who thirsts, come to the waters. And you who have no money, come buy and eat. Yes, come buy wine and milk without money without price...For My thoughts are not your thoughts nor are your ways mine. As the heavens are above the earth, so My ways are above yours."
Isaiah 55

The very word deserve is an annulment of the word serve. When we give and receive not from a sense of entitlement, but from abundance we have raised our ways a little above the earth. Thank you, Lord, for the gift of this marriage. May I respond with a willingness to serve.

Got Your Back

Marriage is designed to make sure someone has your back. It would be complicated for God to be there to rescue all of us in every circumstance, especially considering how partial He is to anonymity. Not that He would mind us knowing that it is always Him who protects us... it is we grown ups that seem to have an insatiable desire for autonomy. So He invented spouses.

I have a friend facing hip replacement surgery. Think he would let me offer to bring a meal? Not a chance. If I arrive at the door with a casserole he will probably leap from the couch and offer me tea, apologizing that there is no peach pie. Children are not so particular. They accept help like there is no tomorrow, because for them, life is about today.

Just now, my twins were getting ready to go out in the snow and I asked why Aurelle was wearing shoes instead of boots.

"I left them at school."

"But I am going to make big footprints for her to step in," her booted sister assured me.

Kids are comfortable with help, which makes it much easier to help them. Marriage seems to be a plot for breaking through that invincible shield, making it possible to admit to yourself and another human being that you are vincible.

It is snowing and I have to drive in it. My thoughts went something like this.

"I will go up the less steep road, but if I get stuck, I will call John. He will shovel out the car, and I will drive behind in his tire tracks."

John likes rescuing me. I like being rescued.

But for those of you who are sticklers for equanimity, rest assured. When we are in a social situation it is me who does the blazing. John does not thrive on chit chat, and marvels that I can remember not only the coworker's name but her husband's name, their children's names and random details like their oldest son's recent engagement. John will willingly follow along in my verbal footprints.

I think it is much nicer than standing alone.

Happy Birthday

My birthday was coming and I was sure John would forget. I was already building up resentment, three days ahead. The embarrassing thing was, if I had taken time to notice, that John's birthday is on Christmas and has been lost in the shuffle every year. If he was looking to me to set the bar for birthday blazing, it was in the corner somewhere under the couch.

But never mind, I was bent on him remembering this birthday, and with no help from me.

The actual day of my birthday he began making absent

minded inquiries about the van, which was being fixed. We had another smaller car, but he needed the Toyota for some reason. I said it would be ready by four. That seemed to make him edgy, but I was too busy stewing to pay attention. He went to pick up the car late in the afternoon, saying he had an errand to do. Whatever.

When he came home with the car and a very big box, he triumphantly plunked it in the living room. It said Bernina on it. Now Bernina is a company that makes high end sewing machines, ones that I had never even wasted time coveting. But here before me was a Bernina box. I wondered why he had gone to the trouble to get an empty Bernina box to put my present in.

"Open it!" he was clearly excited. Still transitioning from confusion, I looked inside and found a Bernina sewing table! Unbelievable! A place to reign in the unwieldy notions and fabric and pins that spilled over the dining room.

"Now put your sewing machine on it!" he suggested. I ran to fetch my low end machine to set it on the beautiful table, but when I got back there was another Bernina box there instead. Confusion came back. What was this box for?

"Open it!" John prodded, as I clearly looked like one of those hoofed animals who cannot cross a grating.

I was stunned to find an actual Bernina sewing machine inside the Bernina box, on the Bernina table. This could not be mine, on the day that I had gotten a running start of seventy two hours expecting John to forget. I threw my arms around him and in vague terms I apologized for unnamed errant behavior. I thanked him profusely for his extravagance!

Little did we know how extravagant.

The next day the Bernina store called to say there had been a slight discrepancy when they went to close the books at 5 o'clock. They had charged our credit card not $1,200, but $12,000. They would be refunding the difference.

Embers

Our daughter Chara lives in the city now, so we don't see her as much as we used to. She came over last night with Legos for Ben and Clue for the twins. We enjoyed snapping and accusing, and dipping hummus by the fire.

As is par for the course, I went to bed just as Chara was starting round two of her evening's events. Her friends pulled into the driveway and whisked her off into the snowy darkness just as the fire was settling down to a smolder.

This morning I woke up hours before anyone and padded down the carpeted stairs. I turned on lights and cleared the residual dishes. After snuggling under a quilt on the couch I thought I heard a rustling sound. I glanced up at the fireplace and saw orange flames doing a tango behind the grate.

How could the embers have lasted? There were only a few chunks of charcoal left from last night's logs, like buoys in a sea of soot. Eight hours is a long time to hang on to heat.

But there it was, as if it had been waiting for my return.

Recently I spoke with a friend whose marriage had rekindled. Five years ago she told me it was over. After the last child packed up for college, she could not bear the thought of languishing in this blackened relationship any longer. But somewhere between the nighttime of hopelessness and the dawn of new feelings, her affection had sparked. It was not a wild burning, but it was enough to make her pull up a double wedding ring and stay. She and her husband had a partnership. In the pause between regret and dissatisfaction, there were embers of friendship.

She looked up and there was her marriage, as if it had been waiting for her return.

Two Arms

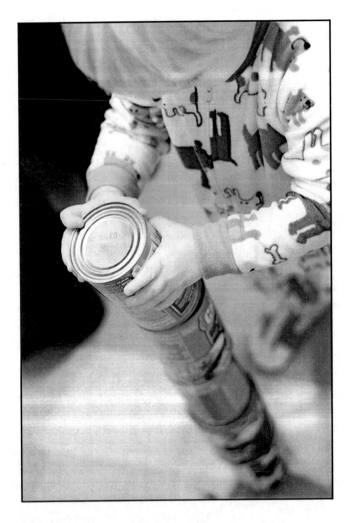

I fell on a slippery slope at a church camp and whacked my poor old bod. The bruise on my thigh was as black as coffee, and in the words of Benjamin looked "scary." But the more pressing concern was the damage to my left forearm. I do not score highly in the intelligence Gardner describes as bodily-kinesthetic but I was certain I should not move it. The improvised sling helped insure that, and I spent the next few days learning to live with one arm.

What struck me first was the people around me who so casually maneuvered two hands. They lifted, grabbed, hugged, clapped, ate, played guitar and carried things easily. The cooperation of two limbs had never seemed so miraculous to me as it did now. The once simple task of holding a plate and filling it with food now took serious planning. Sweeping at chore time was sloppy. Playing for worship was impossible. I tugged out a foot of floss and soon realized it was too hard to keep it taut.

Then I gradually started to figure out ways to still help in the kitchen, and dress. It took attention but I didn't want to simply give up. My right arm did double duty, and I learned how to hold gently with my left hand without actually putting pressure on the arm.

The cooperation of two limbs reminds me of marriage. Working in unison while getting dinner on the table, or paying the bills makes it all much easier. But I know that in our relationship things are often unevenly distributed. John's paycheck is three times what mine is. I spent more time holding babies. I can feel resentful of that inequity, or I can learn to work with it. There have been times when I was incapacitated with asthma, and John took up the slack. Other years he traveled overseas for weeks at a time and I carried the brunt of childcare. What I have finally remembered to remember is that if I begin to feel self righteous about my competence, I can expect to be leaning on him in about ten minutes.

"The two eyes make one sight, the two ears one hearing, the two nostrils one smell, the two lips one speech, the two hands one labor, the two feet one walking, the two hemispheres of the brain one dwelling place of the mind, the two chambers of the heart one life of the body by means of the blood, the two lobes of the lungs one breath. But the masculine and feminine when united in love truly conjugial make one life completely human."

Emanuel Swedenborg, *Conjugial Love* 316

It's Hard

I do not know if this is as difficult as it looks.

Why do people do things that are hard? I have friends who voluntarily climbed Mt Kilimanjaro. On purpose. It not only cost them a chunk of change and time, but it was pretty tough going near the end. Or so they tell me.

I have even heard stories of people who sign up for brutal forms of recreation like crew, or lifting weights. I have never been thus inclined so my reaction includes a generous portion of disbelief.

Last winter I went to a fabulous rendition of Huck Finn, in which the lead never actually left the stage. His dialogues and songs spilled into each other for three hours. How much work went into that production? Did he ever want to quit?

I suppose there is a part of each of us that wants to test our own limits. Can I push my body to run farther, stretch deeper? Can I dig into the pockets of my heart for still more reserves of compassion?

Marriage is hard. But since when is hard a synonym for worthless? Last night was a tough one for John and I. A sick child took a bunch of attention in the predawn hours. But in the morning, when we looked at each other, and knew we had worked together, it felt... well... exhausting.

Sitting side by side with pink lemonade has its merits. But sweating while you plow (or trudge) through your limits feels incredible too.

Graduation

Today is college graduation where I teach.

There are a slew of young adults who have reached a long term goal. It is contagious to see their excitement. They made a plan, years ago, and slogged or shimmied through the steps to get there.

It is part of the human experience to make plans, and to pursue them. Without that capacity we would wander more, own less. Young children do not make plans. They jump with both feet into whatever life offers. It is their mother who signs them up for ballet, or chooses where to go on vacation.

Recently John and I decided to hire a contractor to change the windows in a room that leaks a fair bit of heat in the winter, making it nippy and expensive. I started imagining new ways to enjoy the space, and can already feel the possibilities as well as the work.

Couples can make plans together. One time as we were winding up a marriage group we asked them to create a shared vision and bring it to our last meeting. They each arrived with a written document, and we asked them to read or describe it to the group, so we could support their goals. Everyone did, except one.

They seemed embarrassed, and sullen. We had built a strong sense of community in the weeks we had been meeting and everyone tried to make them feel safe enough to share it. But they refused. It left a sense of incompleteness to our final evening.

But a year later we were surprised to receive a letter from that couple. They had been too ashamed to read their goals because they seemed completely unattainable. Yet they had put them up where they could read them daily. Slowly, they started to move forward in making the dream a reality. They never told us what the plan was, but they did share their joy at achieving it. The couple even celebrated by going to a fancy hotel for the weekend, and toasting their success by the beach.

You can make a dream. Whether you are already married or not, whether you are content or frustrated, you have the capacity to imagine where you would like to be, in four years or forty. Quite likely the journey will include slogging, jumping, and doubt. But I invite you to go ahead and perch it on your wall where you can see it, and to make steps every day.

And if you let me come to your party I promise to bring a present.

The Third Side of Conflict

The other day we went out for lunch with a couple we love. It was a friendly hour, chatting about our lives.

Then they looked at each other as if on cue.

"Shall we ask about... you know...?"

They launched into a conflict about how to spend their next anniversary. Should it be an international venture, or one closer to home? Should they leave the kids for a shorter time, or splurge for two weeks? She laid down her reasons for long and far, like bricks in the path. Then he gave his well laid rationale for shorter and closer. I think they wanted us to vote. I was not sure if that would require us to donate to the trip.

We listened and tried to reflect their heart felt motivations. But we did not take sides.

Recently I found a chart called the Third Side of Conflict. It unravels the ways we can place a transitional energy between two diverging sides. There are mediators, peacekeepers, witnesses, bridge builders. It reminds me of what little I know about connective tissue, that enables my forearm to swivel up while my upper arm points down, without becoming dismembered.

What I became aware of as they were speaking, was the love between the two of them. They were in perfect agreement that they were eager to spend time together. Their love shone over every choice.

Together close
Together far
Together long
Together short

I don't know how they will celebrate their next milestone. But I rejoice that they will do it together.

I think I will send a donation.

Hiking

This is the brand of a Boy Scout Leader who hiked Philmont. It is among the most arduous challenges in scouting, held in the high mountains of New Mexico. The wearer of the boot led a dozen scouts for 50 miles through rugged terrain. When a crew of boys and fathers arrive at the high camp, they are welcomed by a ranger who is well versed in the rigors of the trail. He travels with them for a day or two, to be sure they are savvy about bear ropes and water purification tablets.

I had seen teenagers walking around town in the weeks

before they flew to Philmont, hefting a back pack and building up stamina. They had fundraisers all year to help cover the cost of food and equipment. The program has a very impressive success rate. There are clear expectations spelled out before you arrive, and skilled park staff poised to guide you away from trouble. Commissaries are strategically placed throughout the camp, so that crews can replenish supplies every few days.

A WAMI plaque is awarded to every crew whose members all finish the hike. It stands for We All Made It. The sense of teamwork is paramount to the success of each person.

But there is no substitute for putting one foot in front of the other.

It is not a stretch of the imagination to believe there were grueling miles on hot afternoons. Back packing is not for wimps. I can believe there were silent tears shed in the darkness of a two man tent, when they finally laid their packs down and felt the droning ache of a body pushed to its limit. When your boots are pinching, or your hamstrings are pulled, it is hard to muster the energy to keep trudging. Hiking sounds like a cool adventure when you are looking at the website, or hearing about the wildlife. But reading about it and showing up mile after dirty mile exist in entirely different dimensions.

Marriage success rates are not yet as lofty. But I believe we can put strategies in place to change that. A dozen mentors are being trained to welcome younger couples along the path, and to help them find their footing. Commissaries, in the form of marriage groups, conferences and online support keep couples refueled. Many couples are involved in premarital counseling, to educate themselves about the road ahead.

But there is no substitute for putting one foot in front of the other.

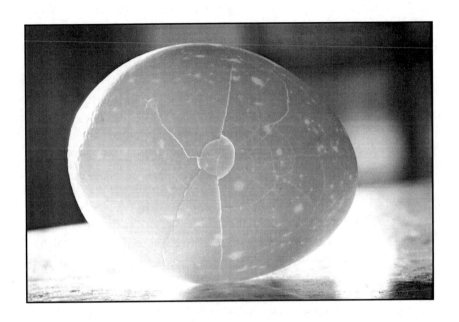

Cracked But Not Shattered

I remember thinking my father was perfect. He was my hero, and my eyes were blind to any flaws in his character. But gradually, I reluctantly looked at some of his choices, and my adoration stalled. Perhaps getting in the car mid fight with my mother and driving three hundred miles to cool off was not an impeccable decision, but it was the best he could manage.

Those were the first cracks in my image of him. I was after all the little girl who was left behind with the manic mother. My hero did not rescue me.

Yet decades later, I find myself face to face with my own imperfections. My child has a condition that renders logic obsolete. Autism hijacks his ability to calm down in a storm, or when the computer crashes. So when I mentally go away, albeit only in the next room, I remember the image of my father slamming the car door. For him, leaving was a better choice than duking it out with a woman in an altered mental state. I can forgive him for that crack in his armor, and it helps me understand what I could not fathom at the tender age of twelve. He was human, and had reached his breaking point.

I had expected to be a perfect wife and mother, one who had unlimited resources of patience and compassion. But that dream did not come true. I have said and felt things that I never would have predicted, and faced my own shattered image.

Yet I suppose the cracks in an eggshell are the only way the chick can come out into the sunlight.

Look Behind You

Benjamin is kind of vulnerable to teasing. Not that he cares what you think of him but he has limited social awareness about how to stay out of harm's way. Fortunately, (a word he likes to use when he can fit it in) he has six older siblings who are often right behind him. Even if they do not need to intervene, the presence of a six foot older brother or eyebrows furrowed sister are enough to deter a would-be taunting ten year old who does not understand autism. Benjamin does not even realize it but they have his back.

I will admit it right up front. I believe those stories about angels and miracles, interceding in ordinary life. I have several books about earthlings being blessed by angels and I know many of the vignettes by heart.

In one of them a woman was working with inner city teenagers and was locking up the door late at night. A crowd of surly kids surrounded her and she was scared. She prayed. Then the crowd dispersed suddenly and she could hurry safely to her car.

Later she asked one of the kids why they had left her alone. "When those big guys in white showed up we were not about to mess with you." Huh? What guys in white? Was there... could it have been...

Sometimes we are fooled by thinking that the only things to be seen are the things we can see. It reminds me of when no one bought the notion of germs because they were invisible to the naked eye, or Galileo was arrested for saying that the earth revolves around the sun, which was not how it looked to the average 16th century astronomer.

But I believe with everything in me that there is more going on than my two blue eyes can tell me about. On occasion the veil lifts and we glimpse the splendor of substances that are infinitely more lasting than the clutter in front of me. I may have my attention locked on the problem which looms large in my marriage, but even if I am inadequate to the task... there are angels hovering just behind me that are. I am too slow to whip around and catch them, but if I keep very still I can hear their soft murmuring.

"Do not fear, for those who are with us are more than those who are with them." And Elisha prayed, and said, "LORD, I pray, open his eyes that he may see." Then the LORD opened the eyes of the young man, and he saw. And behold, the mountain was full of horses and chariots of fire all around Elisha.

2 Kings 6:16

Speak For Yourself

The other day on NPR I heard a woman being interviewed about some topic which escapes me. What stuck however was her sweeping comment.

"I am from the west. People in the east may want .... but those of us who live in the west don't."

Really? Does she actually thinks she can be a spokesperson for an entire coast? Two coasts in fact?

I sometimes hear people edit their own words mid sentence.

"My wife and I.... excuse me, let me speak for myself, I would like to come. I will check with her."

This is a good thing. Always. (catch that sweeping statement?)

Although I have a lengthy history with John, and my kids, and my siblings, something freezes when I believe there are no more surprises. Do I actually think I have paid close enough attention to predict all future interactions? Good grief, I still surprise myself. It is not as if any of us are made of metal and never change.

It is a choppy transition to go from the dictatorial state of early parenting to the gradual introduction of choice for young children. Personally I have bungled it on numerous occasions.

"You did not want to have a playdate? Sorry, I already invited her."

"You don't want piano lessons? Oops, I already paid through December."

Other times my kids are annoyed that I cannot predict their wishes.

"Mooom, you know I always want my burrito with cheddar, corn, beans and olives on a corn tortilla, but Hope wants them with white cheese, guac, rice and salsa on a wheat one!" I am glad they think I am that smart.

Zack took matters into his own hands. He made a note on my phone about exactly how he prefers his burritos. He can even edit it as the need arises.

Thanks, Mom

My son Zack asked me to make sure he woke up this morning at six. Part of me wanted to "forget", since it was for a lacrosse game three hours away, where the temperature would be in the thirties. Not only that he would have to wait on the sidelines for the varsity game too, making the whole shebang a twelve hour escapade on a day Zack normally sleeps in until noon.

But the phone call up to his room on the third floor was forever sweetened by two words.

"Thanks, Mom." Thanks??? For waking him in the dark to dress in three layers of sweats to ward off the cold while he smacks his hands together on a frosty field north of Scranton? If he does not get to play for more than three minutes my inner Mother Bear is going to wake up from hibernation.....

But wait. He said "Thanks, Mom."

Which reminds me of the day he got four teeth yanked in preparation for a masked stranger strapping a version of barbed wire across his teeth. His mouth was oozing gauze and blood, but he still managed to say, "Thank you," to the antagonist with the pliers. In fact he said it three times.

Let's review. He is a sixteen year old boy. All the developmental psychology books label this period as one of rebellion, lack of respect for authority, withdrawal from parental influence. So how is it that he manages to soften my experience of life with those two words? Isn't it my job to sweeten his life?

Although I was glad to hear his appreciation when I bought him a new lacrosse stick last week, it was less surprising. But when I hear those words after waking him at dawn, or a messy ordeal with the oral surgeon... I am transported to a place I do not often run to.

Gratitude is a contagious condition. When I am gifted with appreciation, it births kindness within me. I watch it spread as I amble along my ordinary way. After Zack has spontaneously thanked me, I let drivers in ahead of me. I greet the post lady with a smile. I am friendly to the teller at the bank.

All because a sleepy teenager said "Thanks, Mom."

What's In a Name?

I have a friend who sprinkles the name of the person she is speaking to into the dialogue. It sounds seamless, and yet the novelty of it still swells my heart rate a notch. It is silly, I suppose, to feel special. Of course she knows my name, yet to hear her natter it is another imprint of our friendship.

My children call me Mom. Like a chameleon the word takes on the color of the message, whether it is a request, or a reminder, a complaint or a caress. I love to hear John voice my name when we are together. Unfortunately, though, somewhere along the way I began to associate my name spoken at a higher decibel with being in trouble. He will yell across the house.

"Lori!!!"

"What did I do?" the response comes faster than my frontal lobe can edit it, even though John has told me that he does not want me to go straight to Reprimand.

But when we are side by side, and he speaks that single word, I feel chosen.

I have tried to use the knowledge to help him feel hand picked too, rather than hen pecked.

"John, how did you sleep?"

"How did the meeting go, John?"

A name is brazen enough to try to wrap its four or eight letters around a human spirit like a house tries to encompass a family, or a painting attempts to capture a sun washed landscape.

John.

John.

John...

Bungee Jumping

Christmas is a season of extremes.

When I go walking after a new snowfall the silence suggests that there might not be another living soul for miles. The solitude surrounds me as far as I can see. Then if I concede to take three daughters to the mall the cacophony and crowds convince me that there has been a global migration to this particular store. Signs and price tags all skew my sense of balance until I begin to believe that $148 is a steal for a sequined mohair sweater, and how have I managed to sustain meaningful life without one?

Then I break free of that magnetic monetary force field and head for the parking lot. The timid tinkling of the Salvation Army Santa pulls my awareness back to the portion of humanity for whom any sweater at all, stained and second hand, would bring precious warmth.

December is peppered with parties, and I can feel the joy of marriage and family in an embarrassment of riches. So many jovial friends in every variation of red apparel, bearing sugar sprinkled cookies and wrapped surprises, bringing laughter and love in abundance. There are more bodies than I can hug, more truffles than I can swallow.

But around the corner there is probably someone feeling desperately alone. The absence of connection stings even more sharply in juxtaposition to the lights and music spilling out of the windows next door.

My mother is getting older. The wrinkles on her hands now outnumber the smooth places, and the struggle to move her body from one resting place to another often outweighs the motivation to get there. Carrying accessories takes a toll on her limited endurance, so she asks for help or goes without. Yet daily she welcomes my sprightly daughters who love to dance at her feet and twirl pretty necklaces. Their whole life spans less time than their grandmother spent in college six decades ago. For them movement is as necessary as breathing, and extra dolls and flowers improve the journey.

It is a stretch to be yanked from one end of the spectrum to another. It feels like bungee jumping. Solitude and crowds, decadence and dearth, lavishness and lack, longevity and new life.

When I try to squeeze into an awareness of the circumstances of Jesus' birth, I notice a similar disparity. Evidently Bethlehem was packed beyond capacity. Mary and Joseph must have felt the angst of being unwanted and isolated. Even my best efforts at self pity pale against such rejection. Yet there were other people, people of great import, who not only desired the company of this wee family, they were determined to invest significant time and expense to obtain it. Boinnng.

The shepherd's nightly vigil was a lonely one. Likely the only sounds on the hill were the soft bleat of sleepy sheep and the scant light was from the campfire. Then in an explosion of brightness and song came a canopy of angels, obliterating all traces of feeling alone or forgotten. Heaven itself yanked them from fear and doubt to its burnished threshold. Booiiinngg.

The celestial message was of peace. For a moment suspended in time humankind gazed across the veil into reality where pain's tenacious fingers could not reach. Then just as abruptly, the heavy threat of infanticide sent the couple into the darkness, racing for the Life of a Baby. Boooiiinnggg.

Rejection and worship, monotony and exultation, exile and peace. Why the incessant paradox? Where is the illusive balance? Wouldn't it be simpler to just settle for mediocrity somewhere in the middle?

It would appear that God wants something more.

There is considerable energy stored up in a bungee rope stretched to its limit. The force is invisible until it is unleashed, when we witness our own sweeping acceleration toward something that seconds ago felt pathetically out of reach.

Christmas can be a tromping ground for greed, frenzy and depression. Yet in another breath we can be grabbed bodily and transported by a Cord whose zenith is fixed to the brightest Star in the sky.

Vulnerable

Vulnerability is the birthplace of connection.

So says Brené Brown, a smart woman whose TED presentation about a virtue that outclasses brains has five and a half million views. Of course, if I am any indication perhaps it is only a million because I have watched it five and a half times.

Brené interviewed thousands of people about shame and vulnerability. In the process of trying to analyze human connection she found that the people who are most joyful, are also willing to be authentically flawed.

Our culture is perhaps more obsessed with numbing our inadequacies than any in history. We manipulate our bodies, our moods, our bank accounts, our persona in a relentless chase for perfection. Addictions, plastic surgery, stimulants, obsessive spending are driven by a need to be seen as worthy.

Yet the very prize we seek is an arm's length away. We can pull down the masks obscuring us from the people we live with. We can dare to be vulnerable.

The three most significant hours I ever spent with my own brother and sisters was when a therapist guided us to answer a deceptively simple question.

If they were to really know you at your core, what would they see?

Marriage is an invitation to be vulnerable. It is a sacred opportunity to be skin to skin with another bruised and aching body.

After a lifetime of bungling, and fleeing from mistakes, we arrive where we began that day at the altar. We believe we are enough.

Looking Closely

I bet they are all around you even now, and you didn't see them. You walked into the room, sat down and never noticed. It takes energy to look. It requires a deep desire to find them, even when they are inconspicuous.

There are green things surrounding you. I started hunting and found fifty seven and I have not yet even put on my glasses. Some are turquoise, or sage, forest or apple. They were there whether or not I turned my head, though I think their color brightened at my gaze. I laughed to realize I had missed two on first inspection... the rug under my feet and the print of the skirt I am wearing.

Blessings are all around us too, though we get stale at remembering. It is a pity, really, because the joy is intensified with awareness. The birds were singing just now, heedless of my attention, but when I became receptive the sound pierced my calloused senses. I wonder what happens to the joy when I am too passive to pick it up? Does it wait for another blessee more open than me? Or is there a cache predestined for me alone, and if I neglect it it atrophies?

There are blessings in your marriage, even if you are not yet wed. The blessings come wrapped in hope, and relationships that are honing your ability to listen and forgive. It is a wondrous gift, the chance to bump up against an ornery person and learn the skill of compassion. The gratitude comes later, when experience softens the friction between you and your spouse. Sometimes you remember.

"I am able to be patient now, because of that rascally co worker after college."

More often we don't.

It helps to have a companion in the search. John and I are scribing them in a journal together. The intention to find them helps creak open my sights to the ubiquitous.

A woman named Ann Voskamp who is homeschooling her six children on a farm in Canada is jump-starting my sense of blessings. In her book, *One Thousand Gifts*, she has a playful list of what to look for. I enjoyed the scavenger hunt.

Grrr

I have heard it said that there are only four core emotions, and anger is not one of them.

Anger may just be a scary mask for a more fragile feeling, like sadness.

I am not sure who gets to decide such things, but I know that for years raising little kids I could not quite tease out my own knee jerk response when one of them was hurt. I got mad.

Why was that? A child runs to me in tears, having catapulted herself off the couch and landed in a pile of Lincoln logs. She is bruised and wants a hug, yet I feel compelled to deliver a stern lecture on the importance of safety and the avoidance of unnecessary risks.

Awareness of this ridiculous response was the first step toward changing it, though I must admit I am still not exactly Florence Nightingale.

I remember times when I would send my little boy to his room for a minor misdemeanor and he would say "I hate you!" I think his words were a thin veneer for "I want to be close to you. Being far away makes me sad."

Then there was the "You are late!" period in our matrimonial progression, or should I say regression. John would neglect to call and tell me where he was, and I went through a cycle that launched with anger, morphed into fear, shifted to a fantasy about my life as a widow with a litter of small children, and slid back to anger again. If he walked in during the livid part of the not so merry go round, my face said "Grrr!" but I suspect my heart was frozen by fear.

Why was it so impossible to just say, "I was terrified that you were dead! I LOVE YOU! I never want to lose you!"

I guess because, in terms of eternity, I am still just a little girl.

Inside

Inside a puddle is a splash waiting to be set free.
Inside your arms is a hug waiting to be given.
Inside your lips is a smile waiting to be offered.
Inside your throat is a kind word hoping to be spoken.

Source

It seems like love originates from us.

The surge of energy popping through our hearts shows up like internal fireworks, and then settles down to a wood stove warmth. There are no visible tubes, chutes or wires attached to an outside source, so, obviously, the love comes from within.

But some things are not what they appear. I could also try to nab credit for the increased temperature of my skin when I lounge by the pool on a sizzling July day. There were no external indicators to suggest otherwise. I might applaud myself for a sharp shift in emotions when I arrive at a friend's wedding in a cross condition, and soften to hear Gabriel's Oboe played beautifully.

I continue the illusion when I suggest that the lack of love means that the source has dried up.

Hogwash.

The Source of love is not so fickle as that. What if I were to stay in an overly air conditioned room, cursing the frigid day, refusing to step through the glass door and into the ninety degree air?

Imagine my folly if I chose to stay in the lady's room during that wedding of dear friends, fussing with my recalcitrant stockings, out of earshot of any music or sacred promises, and whined at the reception about how mediocre the service was?

If I am cold and grouchy, it is not because the supply of sunshine and congeniality are exhausted. It is because I am, sometimes with great effort, staying away from them.Inside a puddle is a splash waiting to be set free.

It's All Good

Yesterday John's parents pulled into the driveway. I was not expecting them but I rose to greet them. They had trouble finding somewhere to sit in the living room, as I was in a flurry of quilt-making and the couches had been converted to viewing surfaces.

"We can only stay a minute. We are on our way to a luncheon. But I wanted to tell you that everything is good. Everything that happens leads to happiness, even the things that look bad." My father in law seemed emphatic.

Had he seen the news about Aurora? Was he aware of the pending laws giving Monsanto immunity? Did he realize that people I love are out of work?

"Things that appear terrible are there to make you stronger." He paused to offer a melon shaped smile in lieu of an exclamation point. I glanced at his wife of sixty years. She nodded, heavy with memory.

They are closer to ninety than to eighty, and have seen enough heartache to use up a box of tissues. Or three. Dad fought in WWII at the age my sons were shooting animated bad guys on a 3 inch screen, a bag of chips at the ready. He tried for decades to invent and produce erasers that would saturate the market, and watched his beloved business go bankrupt, taking two houses with it. He had felt the irreconcilable gap between his father and brother cleave their family over religious differences.

"Even divorce. You can write that in your, uh, newspaper. After monopolizing the entire conversation I have to go. Rachel." She stood as if her name had been the tap of a baton and her husband was the conductor. We hugged and they left for their engagement.

I mulled over the one specific of his monologue. Three of their grandchildren divorced after less time than he had spent in camouflage. This pithy message, delivered by a man who is in the queue for heaven, was one of urgency to calm down.

Perhaps it is a response. I have been praying lately, for marriages, for unborn babies, for people who have lost the script of their lives. Maybe God grabbed the person next in line to leave me who still has a voice I can hear, to toss me those three words.

It's all good.

About the Author

Lori and her husband John have been involved with marriage support through writing, groups and an annual conference. They have nine children and are grateful for the numberless blessings of parenting together. They also have a music ministry and have composed over a hundred Christian songs.

Visit their website at www.caringformarriage.org.

Photo Credits

Many thanks to all of these
wonderful photographers:

"In Love," p. 12—photo by Jenny Stein
"Buttons," p. 14—photo by Jenny Stein
"Fire Spinning," p. 16—photo by Chara Odhner
"Carrots," p. 18—photo by Andy Sullivan
"Wishing," p. 20—photo by Jenny Stein
"Really?," p. 22—photo by Jenny Stein
"Colly," p. 24—photo by Chara Odhner
"Sleep My Love," p. 26—photo by Chara Odhner
"Just a Juice Box," p. 28—photo by Chara Odhner
"The Tail," p. 30—photo by Chara Odhner
"Something Good," p. 32—photo by Chara Odhner
"Cable Knits," p. 34—photo by Chara Odhner
"Meet Me at the Cafe," p. 36—photo by Andy Sullivan
"Training Wheels," p. 38—photo by Jenny Stein
"Back From the Office," p. 40—photo by Chara Odhner
"Call Me," p. 42—photo by Jenny Stein
"Slipping Away," p. 44—photo by Jenny Stein
"The Veil," p. 46—photo by Jenny Stein
"Turtle," p. 48—photo by Jenny Stein
"Spaces," p. 50—photo by Andy Sullivan
"Darkness Everywhere," p. 52—photo by Andy Sullivan
"Morning Glory," p. 54—photo by Chara Odhner
"Worn Out," p. 56—photo by Jenny Stein
"Scrabble," p. 58—photo by Chara Odhner
"Actress," p. 60—photo by Jenny Stein
"The Only Way Up Is Down," p. 62—photo by Andy Sullivan
"Eat Your Vegetables," p. 64—photo by Jenny Stein
"Making Tigers," p. 66—photo by Chara Odhner
"Rapunzel," p. 68—photo by Jenny Stein
"Outnumbered," p. 70—photo by Andy Sullivan
"Wizard of Oz," p. 72—photo by Jenny Stein
"Help," p. 74—photo by Jenny Stein
"On the Other Side of Won't," p. 76—photo by Jenny Stein
"Washable," p. 78—photo by Chara Odhner